BLURS, SHIFTS
& EDGES

STUDIO AS BOOK
NO. 08

SERIES INTRODUCTION

Studio as Book is a series of publications that tender the extraordinary creative work undertaken in the School of Architecture + Cities design studios – in detail. Each book in the series covers the work of a single design studio, either undergraduate or graduate, and sometimes both, over the course of at least two years. Its objectives are:

- To record, archive, and present the pedagogical programme and creative student outputs of a design studio.
- To position the work of a design studio within a broader intellectual, scientific or aesthetic field.
- To advance the design driven research being undertaken in the School's design studios.
- To provide a reference for future iterations and variations of a design studio.

Compressing the creative output of a multi-year design studio into a single volume, using a pre-designed book template is no easy undertaking, and it is necessarily selective. At the same time, it provides a consistent, sure platform for the wide range of approaches to the discipline of teaching architectural design which characterise the school.

Each Studio as Book has been peer-reviewed on the basis of a proposal submitted by the studio's tutors to an editorial committee. In addition to studio briefs and student work, each book includes content that draws out the studio's research and pedagogical agenda. The format that this takes varies from book to book – reflective essays by tutors or past students, interviews, theoretical essays from parallel fields, and so forth.

I wish to acknowledge the contribution of the following in bringing this project to fruition: Lindsay Bremner, Director of Research and Knowledge Exchange, who was the driving force behind the series when it was launched in 2016; Mark Boyce, author of Sizes May Vary, A workbook for graphic design (Lawrence King, 2008) – and the designer of Studio as Book; Filip Visnjic and Mirna Pedalo, who have given the books a presence on OpenStudiowWestminster: http://www.openstudiowestminster.org/studio-as-book/; and the design tutors and students who have given of their time and energy to collate and edit the books into this unique series.

Harry Charrington
Former Head of the School of Architecture + Cities
University of Westminster

BLURS, SHIFTS & EDGES

DESIGN STUDIO 04
EDITED BY PAOLO ZAIDE & TOM BUDD

STUDIO AS BOOK
NO. 08

SCHOOL OF ARCHITECTURE + CITIES
UNIVERSITY OF WESTMINSTER

CONTENTS

PREFACE — 007
Paolo Zaide and Tom Budd

INTRODUCTION: FRAGILE LANDSCAPES — 010
Paolo Zaide

GROUND SURFACE — 018
Christine Hawley

01 PLOTTING

ON PLOTTING — 026
Paolo Zaide and Tom Budd

FORT FOLLOWS FUNCTION — 030
Greg Brookhouse

SACRIFICIAL PLOTS — 038
Reece Murray

ADAPTIVE GROUND — 046
Greg Brookhouse

CLIFFE MARSHLANDS — 058
Reece Murray

02 STAGING

ON STAGING — 072
Paolo Zaide and Tom Budd

MALLEABLE LANDSCAPES — 076
Colin Walters

CONVERSATIONS — 086
Tom Budd with former Studio 4 students
Adelina Ivan, Axelle Sibierski, Ioana Zavoianu, Marta Contente, Pablo Pimentel

COLLECTIVE HARVEST Adelina Ivan	100
SOUTHEND STAYPORT Pablo Pimentel	112
WINDRUSH CAPITAL Fenn Wright	124
PHOTO ESSAY: WAYS OF WORKING	136

03 SPECULATION

ON SPECULATION Paolo Zaide and Tom Budd	172
CYBERPLACE IN THE METAVERSE Bodhi Horton	176
TOMORROW'S IMAGE FACTORIES Eric Turner	184
A NEW DECENTRALAND Bodhi Horton	192
A LUDDITE FALLACY Eric Turner	204
ENDPAPER Susannah Hagan	219
BIOGRAPHIES AND ACKNOWLEDGEMENTS	221

PREFACE

PAOLO ZAIDE & TOM BUDD

"There was the red sun, on the low level of the shore, in a purple haze, fast deepening into black; and there was the solitary flat marsh; and far away there were the rising grounds, between which and us there seemed to be no life, save here and there in the foreground a melancholy gull."

This passage from Charles Dickens's *Great Expectations* captures the atmosphere of the Thames Estuary, a landscape we returned to again and again over the course of three years. Each October, we set off at first light to explore a different part of the estuary and returned west to the city as the sun began to fall. Central to these trips were long walks: from Gravesend to the Cliffe Marshes, Canvey Island to Southend, and Tilbury Town to Grays. These walks allowed us to slow down, to sense the tidal shifts along the river's edge, and to look out towards a horizon widely captured in narrative, art, and popular culture. Over the three years, we moved through readings, drawings, projects, and pauses. This book is one such pause: A moment to look back at our first walk and to consider where the studio might head next.

To frame the book's central ideas, we are honoured to include contributions from Christine Hawley and Susannah Hagan, whose perspectives on architecture, teaching, and the environment have informed our work over many years. Christine Hawley's opening essay explores the process of translating concepts into drawings and buildings, highlighting how this experimental journey remains 'opaque' or blurred. Her writing reveals the dynamic interplay between the built and unbuilt, the material and immaterial, showing how ideas can transform as they take shape. Susannah Hagan concludes the book by addressing a pressing question: how are climate change, urbanisation, and ecology reshaping the way we should teach architectural design today? She reminds us that designers must once again engage with the metabolic, as well as the social and formal, dimensions of cities. Her think piece underscores how environmental engineering and natural systems design can - and should - become central forces in reimagining 21st-century urbanism. Their reflections offer valuable context and insight, linking broader questions to the specific ground we walked. Their voices frame the work we developed in the studio and remind us of the importance of sustained dialogue across time, disciplines, and shifting landscapes.

While design and environmental change remained ongoing themes in our studio, the work produced during this period reflects a moment of transition. Returning to the physical studio after prolonged digital isolation raised key questions: How can we reconnect with space, with each other, and with shared ways of working? Students had to re-engage with the spatial, social, and collaborative processes that are foundational to the architectural studio. At the same time, we observed a broader shift from tactile modes of designing to more digitally mediated ways of working. Rebuilding the studio became a way to respond to shifts unfolding in both the natural and the digital environments.

The estuary became the canvas through which we explored how natural and digital shifts are presented, perceived, and propositionally interacted with. Over three years, we developed a range of design methods: landscape drawing, model and device creation, time-based media, digital visualisation, moving image, and storytelling through visuals. With the estuary as our backdrop, the studio became a space to reflect, test, and exchange new ideas.

We hope this book captures not only the creative energy and risk, but also the speculative spirit that drives the studio forward.

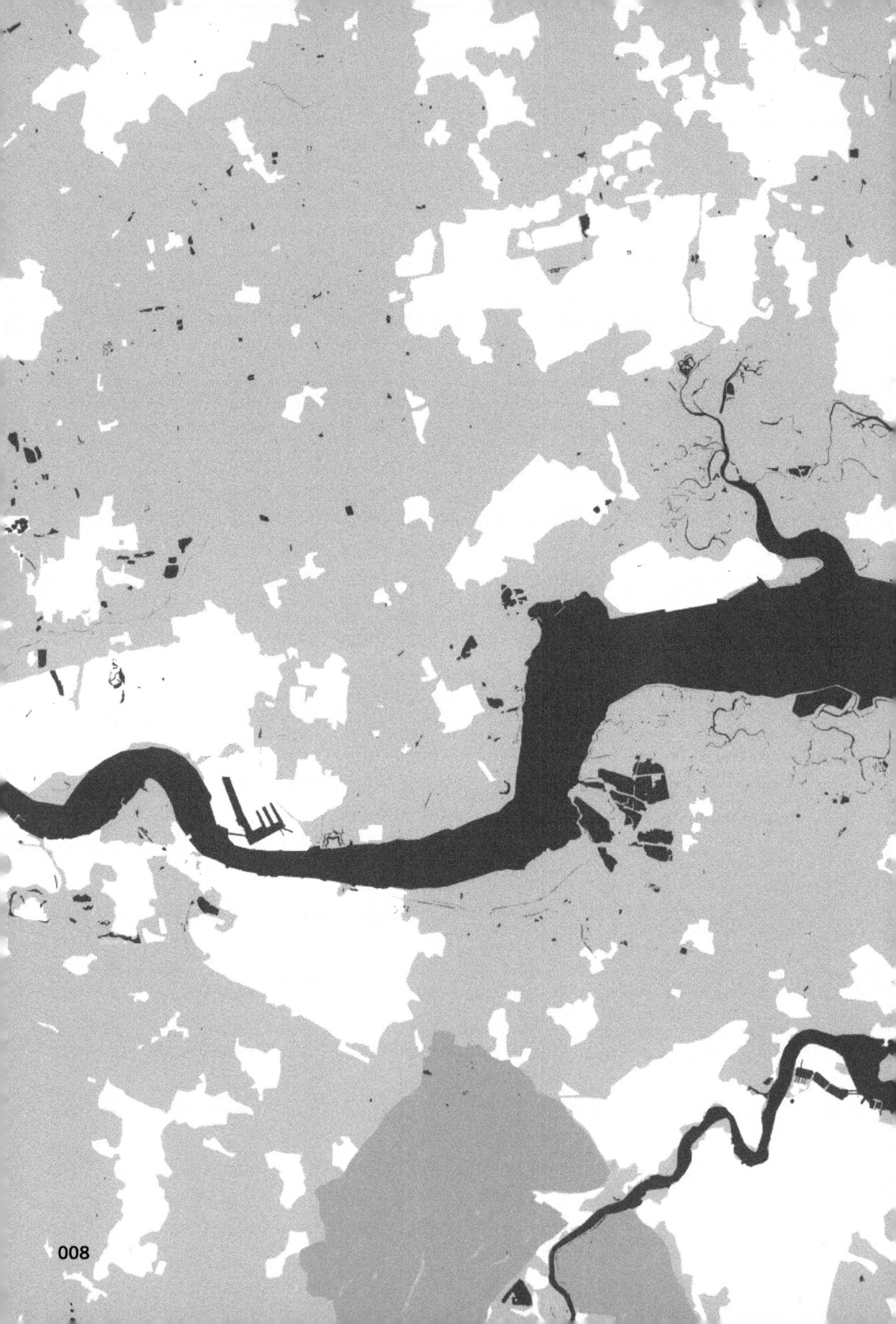

FRAGILE LANDSCAPES

INTRODUCTION

PAOLO ZAIDE

As the prospect of environmental stability slips away and we experience a climate that becomes increasingly volatile, the challenge will be to understand how to provide shelter in this environment. The scenario is set fifty years in the future, which, if the climate pundits are correct, will be a time characterized by increasing storms, drought, and rising sea levels.

In this scenario, how do we consider not only the organisation of communities and the design of places for living, but also the complex network of external services and infrastructure that supports them? Architecture does not exist in isolation; we need to consider context, whether that is urban or in open country. The daily routine of all individuals requires the support by a complex network of external services and infrastructure. With the influence of research, analyses, and speculation, the challenge for architecture students today is to question models of living, and develop infrastructural proposals tested within fragile edge conditions.

This book grew out of the urgent need to reevaluate the design studio and experimental ecological practice in a post-pandemic world. It presents design as a synthetic key, connecting ecology with an urbanism that is not in contradiction with its natural or artificial environment. With much ground covered on the theory of 'ecological urbanism', this book explores its practical application and how it can shape the ethos, methodology, and impact of design teaching.

The pause from the physical studio during the pandemic challenged us to reflect on the impact of a global crisis and consider how human activity is deeply intertwined with both the natural and digital worlds. This reflection served as a catalyst for a new direction. Returning to the studio in autumn 2021, we were able to reconnect with our surroundings and direct our focus toward developing architectural approaches that thoughtfully engage with our global environment across multiple scales, timeframes, and viewpoints.

EDGES

Over a three-year period, our studio explored the fragile edges of the River Thames, focussing on the peripheral towns of Gravesend, Southend-on-Sea and Tilbury as case studies. The UK Government has marked the edges of the Thames Estuary as ground for regeneration and further urbanisation.[01] Connecting Westferry in East London to the Isle of Sheppey, this 70-kilometre stretch has also been described as the Thames Gateway. Once home to many heavy and commercial industries, these lands are characterized by a lack of access to public transport, services, and employment. At the same time, the surrounding farm and wild salt marshlands host some of the country's most fragile ecologies. With tidal flows continuously shifting this landscape, what is this a *'Gateway'* to? [02]

The early nineteenth-century Quaker philanthropists, such as Cadbury and Rowntree, understood that working communities needed far more than merely housing to lead a secure and productive life.[03] Bournville and New Earswick were the influential forerunners of the garden city movement that developed models of mixed development that were conceptually radical yet rooted in ideas about humanity. Reimagining the edges along the Thames Estuary demands a radical approach where urban development and infrastructural plans are not referenced by the status quo but by an imaginative vision of life at the midpoint of the twenty-first century. Not only do we need to consider the social consequences of design, but also the technical challenges of changing weather patterns on fragile landscapes.

The demand for housing architecture and infrastructure is a global issue, and tensions arise when geographic locations are chosen. Cities face the lack of available land, while building in the countryside risks damage to wildlife. Given that the political and economic forces behind these decisions rarely satisfy all interests, the studio sought to develop design approaches for a difficult and fragile terrain, which poses the greatest physical and ethical challenges. The sites at the mouth of the Thames Estuary exemplify this, as they are situated on the edge of the water and are therefore particularly vulnerable to the forces of the weather. To explore these ideas, the studio focused on three specific areas of this edge condition.

Gravesend to the Hoo Peninsula

The atmospheric complexity of the Thames Estuary is vividly captured in the misty terrain of Charles Dickens's *Great Expectations* and in the shifting seascapes of Turner's sketches.[04] Over time, parts of this region have evolved into landing places and shipping ports, yet the North Kent marshes hold a stranger history - from military training grounds and gunpowder production sites to cinematic backdrops in films like Kubrick's *A Clockwork Orange* and *Full Metal Jacket*.[05] Our first site, the Hoo Peninsula, is a fragile ecological zone, marked by a history of industrial and military use. It was once a site for brick and cement production, later an RAF base during the Second World War, and more recently, the centre of a contentious debate over a third London airport. Today, this marshland is a tangled network of watercourses and wetlands, where archaeological traces of its past coexist with a rich diversity of wildlife. Nearby, Gravesend, a town historically shaped by naval and shipbuilding industries, continues to support water-based work and serves as a commuter hub for those at Tilbury Docks.

Canvey Island to Southend

Across the Hoo Peninsula, the Essex resort of Southend-on-Sea was granted city status on 1 March 2022, becoming England's 52nd city.[06] To the east, Southend's city edge stretches along seven miles of coastline, defined by the world's longest pleasure pier to the south and London Southend Airport to the north.[07] To the west, the city gives way to farmlands and the river marshes near Leigh-on-Sea and Canvey Island, fragile ecologies shaped by tidal flows and continuous cultural transformation. As Southend seeks to become a tech hub, garden city, or smart city, its very act of "building" could redefine what it means to be a city at all. Might inspiration be drawn from its deep cultural heritage, from John Constable's revolutionary landscapes or Dickens's storytelling, or from the present-day romantic creeks and blues music of Canvey Island, Britain's own Mississippi Delta?

East to West Tilbury

Further inland, the 1930s Dunton Plotlands[08] reflect a desire for rural retreats and a connection to the natural landscape. Bata Town's concept of '*welfare capitalism*' aimed to provide its workers with improved living conditions, social amenities and opportunities for personal dreams and desires.[09] The publicly owned and state-built New Towns, Harlow and Basildon, were a radical combination of modernist planning and the Garden City tradition. Then there is Wallasea Island, a newly formed wetland habitat and artificial island made from excavated material from London's Crossrail project.[10] The coastline also offers a wealth of seaside towns that are gateways to marshland, wildlife and a tacky taste of candyfloss stuck to the inside of your mouth.

Each of these sites presents unique challenges. One will have to address the full responsibilities of preserving delicate ecologies, while also considering the context of growing towns on the periphery and along the water's edge.

SHIFTS

With accelerated climate and digital change, we must consider what to teach the next generation of architects, and how. The field of architecture has always been considered a holistic endeavour, demanding a wide range of knowledge from those who study it. In *The Ten Books on Architecture*, Vitruvius portrays the architect as a polymath, able to synthesize *firmitas, utilitas*, and *venustas*, and whose comprehensive knowledge must extend to history, politics, mathematics, geometry, nature, and weather. This view does not cast the architect as a singular mastermind but rather highlights that their broad education is what allows them to comprehend how their work is connected to numerous external influences.

Against this backdrop, our question is: what approaches to research and design are necessary for architects to navigate today's natural and digital shifts? The question of which methods and processes to adopt was put to students and tutors alike, and this book offers a window into that ongoing discussion.

There are two main strategies for environmental action in architecture. The first is grounded in the material realities and technological demands of climate change. A scientific study of performance, however, extends beyond just materials and methods to encompass new architectural and urban forms, as well as the ways we live in and use them. This approach primarily focuses on quantifiable metrics.

The second perspective, in contrast, relies on bold and unconventional ideas to activate our collective imagination. It accepts that the environment is always changing and positions architecture to envision the built environment's place in that changing world. Both views expand architecture's conventional scope - one through an engineering lens, the other through a social and cultural one. This suggests that the development of new sensibilities requires productive experimentation, rather than a strategy dictated by what is already known. Imagination, here, is equally vital: it is the catalyst for changing minds, enabling people to see the world from a new perspective and inspiring them to act.

BLURS

The studio employed a methodology that deconstructed traditional binaries, recognising that concepts such as nature and culture or art and science are not opposing forces but interconnected systems. This approach, which resonates with the work of practices like James Corner Field Operations, foregrounds the design of "*fields of texture and effect as opposed to objects*" and "*operating in particular contexts as opposed to simply imposing forms."*[11] By drawing upon a wide range of disciplines, including historical and geographic research, photography, ecology and spatial narratives, the studio generated new provocations and evocative scenarios.

The book is framed by contributions from invited authors Christine Hawley and Susannah Hagan, whose essays shape the discussion around ground[12], landscape and architecture. They highlight that architectural teaching must continue to be both experimental and directed. The students' essays and projects for the estuary reflect this approach. By working across strategic, poetic and speculative designs, the book becomes a collection of ideas that are comprehensive yet specific. In the making of the projects, the studio revisited and reimagined the sites, drawing from a variety of sources and different fields of art and design. The unique capacity of architecture to synthesise diverse information and various methods of working is what makes it a distinct discipline.

Given the vast scale of the estuary, the students needed to work collaboratively. They exchanged ideas on common walks, crossed over between year groups, and collaborated with Landscape Studio 8 at The Bartlett School of Architecture.

The publication - a collection of short essays, photographs, cartographies, project work and reflections from students and collaborators of Studio 4 - explores the conceptual and practical frameworks needed to incorporate ecological thinking into the design process. The studio's approach simultaneously serves as a way of understanding and expanding analogue and digital ecological urbanism strategies. The book is therefore thematically organised into three experimental modes of a design: plotting, staging and speculating on the future of the Thames Estuary.

The first, **Plotting**, is informed by James Corner's work on Landscape Urbanism. It is understood as mapping landscapes not as static entities, but as dynamic, interconnected systems. This approach emphasises understanding the complex relationships and processes that shape a site, aligning with a process-oriented understanding of urban environments.

The second, **Staging**, refers to the deliberate interventions into landscapes to facilitate specific experiences, interactions and connections. This concept underscores the architect's role in curating environments that actively shape human behaviours and cultural activities, effectively 'setting the stage' for social engagement.

The third and final section, **Speculating**, draws from the work of Dunne and Raby and frames design to challenge assumptions and create plausible, alternative futures. This approach employs provocative scenarios to spark debate about the ethical and political issues surrounding digital advances. By presenting these *'what-if'* scenarios, **Speculating** encourages critical debate about the kind of future people want (or do not want), shifting the conversation around design from a technical problem-solving exercise to a broader cultural and social discussion.

Collectively these sections aim to bind together design methods and forms of experimentation that project the formation of a new architect into practice. The work ultimately seeks to bridge the towns and landscapes of the estuary, reimagining how climate and digital change might shape the spaces and communities along the Lower Thames Corridor. What will be important for these communities – and how will a hybrid of nature, technology and space support our lifestyles beyond the purely functional? How can this approach help us reconnect to the historic past, the societies of today, and the ecologies and architecture of tomorrow? The ideas presented in this book offer an opportunity to consider how we might engage with these physical and virtual realities. The Thames Estuary presents a site for sensitive investigation, transforming Dickens' *'dark flat wilderness'* into a foggy landscape of wonder and a taste for the unknown.

Notes

(01) UK Department for Communities and Local Government, *Thames Gateway Planning Framework* (London: DCLG, 2005).
(02) "Thames Gateway," *National Archives*, accessed August 20, 2021, https://www.nationalarchives.gov.uk/.
(03) Margaret Richardson, *Quaker Philanthropy and the Garden City Movement in Britain* (York: Quaker Press, 2010).
(04) Charles Dickens, *Great Expectations*, chap. 1 (London: Chapman & Hall, 1861); J. M. W. Turner, Thames Estuary Sketches (1810–20), Tate Britain collection.
(05) Paul Garnham, "Kubrick and the Kent Marshland," *British Film Locations Journal* 12, no. 3 (2015): 45–60.
(06) Department for Levelling Up, Housing & Communities, "City Status Granted to Southend-on-Sea," press release, March 1, 2022, https://www.gov.uk/government/news/city-status-granted-to-southend-on-sea.
(07) Airports Commission, *Final Report* (London: Airports Commission, 2015), 256–60.
(08) John Davis, Plotlands: *Life on the Edge of Urban London* (Basildon: Essex Folklore Publications, 2008).
(09) Karel Dedeček, Bata's *Welfare Capitalism in Britain: The East Tilbury Experience* (Prague: Bata Museum Press, 2002).
(10) RSPB, *Wallasea Island Wild Coast Project – Project Overview* (London: RSPB, 2018).
(11) James Corner, *The Landscape Imagination: Collected Essays 1990–2010* (Princeton, NJ: Princeton Architectural Press, 2014).
(12) Christine Hawley, *Transitions: Concepts + Drawings + Buildings* (Burlington, VT: Ashgate, 2013).

GROUND SURFACE

CHRISTINE HAWLEY

The relationship of architecture to the ground is fundamental not only in a physical sense but in that it demands an awareness of history and how elements have forged reciprocal relationships. The land is a rich source of cultural references that has allowed writers, painters and filmmakers to appropriate both the spectacle and its poetic concepts. It offers a medium of translation, which has great potential to deliver insight into the meandering route of the imagination. The ground as a tool of evocation provides reference that moves from mythology to social iconography, with the capacity to carry a complex implicit narrative The land and its associations use personal narratives and the evocation of memory but it is also a place of death. The land is both a physical reality but, more interestingly, it is also a construct of our imagination. We look at it with our eyes but we use other senses to interpret and create a relationship with 'place' that is quite unique. This essay aims to connect discussions of the ground, where an association with the etymology of the land (scape) has shaped the thinking around a spatial project.

There is an arc of reference often used that engages with topography, historic landscape and the garden, where the translation of critical characteristics with their numerous syntactical similarities is arguably easier to appropriate than other metaphorical or allegorical language. The projects to which this essay refers reflect on the associative nature of land/garden; these oneiric and exploratory proposals are as much a product of unconscious affinities as they are of direct literary reference. The projects contain a fascination with the micro vocabulary of ground, illustrating how the textual and visually visceral play an important part in propelling ideas forward.

There is a long and deep history of land representation in classical art and literature and, more recently, the philosophical deliberations of the landscape urbanists have been at the forefront of a contemporary environmental debate. This text does not claim to be either a methodological or ideological declaration, only a statement of awareness, where certain facts or views

---

This text originally appeared in full as: "Ground Surface" in *Transitions: Concepts + Drawings + Buildings*, Christine Hawley, ©2013) by Routledge, p.47

are important because they linger at the forefront of one's consciousness and others are notable by their absence. This cannot be an exhaustive historic review, as these are ubiquitous and have been executed with commendable academic precision. The essay will, however, suggest connections and use observation to raise questions about the nature of influence during the process of design. In some ways this must sound like an apologia, but in my experience there is often no clear linear route from idea to proposition; it is the circuitous bye-ways that are much more interesting. Sources of interest and influence have been wide ranging, including painting, film, installation art, photography and literature; some have been forensically deconstructed and moved into the architectural realm, but many others have just prompted a reflexive response. Methods of representation and physical reality have both been considered equally legitimate forms of influence occasionally the material has metaphorical connotations which produce oblique translation at other times the evidence is direct; more often it is no more than a background suggestion. During the development of some design proposals, primary observation has been used, but this has never excluded the interpretive work of others that over time has provided a cumulative influence, threading its way in and out of each project.

HISTORIC PAINTING

Historically, the cultural significance of land is both complex and manifold; it has been illustrated as a symbol of power at one end of the spectrum and a poetically nuanced symbol of memory at the other. It has been the professional domain of landowners, land workers, planners, landscape architects and gardeners, all with their designated right to intervene for singular or the communal good. Land is inextricably linked with wealth, politics, ethics and environmental and social well-being. Poets, artists, filmmakers and writers all claim the land as their inexorable source of inspiration.

Throughout history, landscape design has embodied and expressed the values of a culture: at times the power of the state, at times the aesthetics of those at a distance from power.[01]

The lexicon of the land or natural surface has repeatedly been interwoven with the language of abstraction and *'land'* has been a vital medium through which artists have explored and produced the earliest forms of representation, illustrating issues of the day. For the urban dweller, painting still arguably offers the most accessible relationship to the countryside. Paintings of the land, distinct from 'landscape paintings', offer us a value-laden world seen through the cultural lens of the moment.

Although the term 'landscape' formally re-entered

the English from the Dutch *'landschap'* in the early eighteenth century, the earliest depictions of the land existed in Minoan, Greek and Roman friezes. Later, in the fifth century, land' was to become a central theme of the Chinese *'shan shui'* paintings. These images showed pure landscape, where only the merest glimpse of human life was detectable. The pseudo-figurative, fictitious landscapes of the *'shan shui'* ink paintings gave way several centuries later to the mythological, monochrome paintings of the 'wang wei' genre. Although the historic status of landscape painting was notably different between Europe and Asia, the iconography shown in Chinese landscape drawing uses complex cultural narrative that was to influence painters many centuries later.

European paintings of the land were initially no more than a historic record and had little cultural status. In contrast, landscape illustration in Asia was held in high regard and its value was based on a prerequisite of imaginative, intellectual narrative. The influence of these very early oriental paintings was not confined to Asia, as the opening of the historic trading routes transported their influence, to be seen many centuries later in Europe. It has been argued that even the romanticised land and cloudscapes of Turner and Constable owe their conceptual stance to the legacy of this early oriental work.

Linguistically the word 'landscape' was originally used to identify a patch of cultivated ground. It was not used to describe an idealised, picturesque vista until the late eighteenth century. The historically diminished status of landscape painting in Europe was further devalued in the eighteenth century as it also lent itself too easily to the recreation of the 'gentleman painter'. It has been argued, however, that the emergence of the idealised 'rustic' landscape painting coincided with the accelerated enclosure of the English countryside, where the acquisition and sequestration of land by the wealthy created a hitherto unrecognised commodity of power. At this time landscape painting was considered a conceit of the wealthy; the paintings were to contain clear social messages, where land was no longer for production, but for the display of wealth and social status.

Images of the land also began to include totemic language used to illustrate epic social struggles, these paintings first emerged in northern Italy, then Flanders, and finally in the politicised manifestos of the Soviet Russia. With few exceptions, illustrations that were to emerge in the late eighteenth and early nineteenth centuries perpetuated an ideological, perhaps mythological, image that masked reality; rural poverty was virtually concealed. Painting the land, therefore, served several functions, the least important of which was figurative representation. Social stratification, wealth, ideology and folkloric fantasy were all found, using land as the interpretive icon. It was therefore the synthesised images containing motifs of symbolic or mythological value that were sought after, and their creators (including painters such as Nicholas Poussin and Claude Lorrain) were no longer regarded as journeymen painters, but now had acquired the status of poet.

CONTEMPORARY REPRESENTATION

The political and social context in which European painting developed was critical and it served as a reminder that much art emerged under the patronage of the Church or the land-owning aristocracy. The role of landscape painting as propaganda or at least as a reflection of society's mores indicated that 'ground' had a translated totemic value. The linguistic style of these paintings undoubtedly influenced future generations; whether the translational agenda was circumstantial or not, similarities can nonetheless be found in both the incipient technique and symbolism emerging in the paintings of the early twentieth century in the work of artists such as Hopper, Diebenkorn and, later, Hockney. Contemporary artists depicted land with a greater degree of abstraction, often resulting in more desolate compositions lacking any human element. Whether these paintings contained figurative or symbolic elements, representational language of the land also began to emerge as a powerful tool of symbol and enigma.

Painters do not have a monopoly on the representation of land and space, of course; film and video artists have tools at their disposal that enable them to create work with equal if not greater resonance, particularly within an architectural context. The power and understanding of an image often lies in the observer's subjective imagination, rather than the explicit message of the author; the challenge then lies in how to observe certain techniques of painters and filmmakers and explore how these could influence an architectural process, technically and conceptually.

Installation artists, sculptors and photographers such as Andy Goldsworthy, Olafur Elliason and Roger Hiorns use an entirely different range of media, creating immersive environments *King Wall* (Goldsworthy 1997), *Melting Ice on Gunnars Land* (Elliason 2008), *Seizure* (Hiorns 2008/9/10). These installations relate to surface, synthetic or otherwise, to create a 'land' or 'surface' scape within the imagination, dominant materials, colour or texture create the spaces, where each installation's ambiguous title acts as a mnemonic guide. The distinction between these constructions and architecture is a lack of pre-ordained functionality. At what point must a physical purpose be ascribed to space and, once assigned, should this limit the boundaries of interpretation? Gary Hill occupies the realm of immersive art through highly sophisticated video technology;[02] installations such as *Crux* (1983-87) and *Tall Ships* (1992) do not represent the usual orthodoxies of landscape, but both pieces suggest a journey through geographic space that is neither occupied nor unoccupied; it is a place of ambiguity. This is achieved through the capacity of video to offer complex 'non-linear narrative that encourage active engagement on the part of the viewer'. In Roland Barthes' terms, Hill's video narratives can be understood as *'writerly texts'*.[03]

The work of these artists has the freedom to use levels of abstraction and disassociation in a way that is certainly more difficult than the technically explicit realm of architecture. The audience is not in a position in these installations to be entirely conscious of either space, the physical reality of the gallery or the virtual reality of the journey and the levels of imaginative engagement will always be an unpredictable response. Paradoxically the observer might be left reflecting on nature and significance; whereas engagement within architectural space (with some exceptions) is normally through functional expediency. In accepting a lesser degree of control the architect needs to search for a means of expression that captures the audience and encourages greater reflection.

The Turkish filmmaker Abbas Kiarostami by contrast, produces films that explore the intimacy of human relationship to the land using techniques that distil the power of evocation. Kiarostami, heavily influenced by the Japanese filmmaker Yasujiro Uzo, developed a form of cinematic minimalism that undertook to describe themes reflecting the land through gradual revelation. His seminal work *Five* (2003) observes the ebb and flow of the water along the Caspian Sea.[04] Filmed with a motionless camera, events drift in and out of focus, the land and the sea are a timeless backdrop and as the film deliberately lacks a constructed narrative, the audience is obliged to interpret these images through association and memory. The architectural challenge faced by capturing aspects of equivalent nuance is to explore ways of refining the conventionally static palette. A possible technique might be found in the eighteenth-century stratagem of the journey through constructed natural space (landscape) which if interpreted architecturally could create a synthetic alternative offering both dynamic and interpretive parallels. There are, of course, many other references in contemporary film where spatial enigma is played out against the backdrop of carefully contrived landscapes. Ozu's *Late Spring* (1949) and *An Autumn Afternoon* (1962) typify the director's minimal style, suggesting a complexity of narrative through the emptiness of the land. Ozu's obsession with composition and its power to evoke are seen in the opening shots of *Floating Weeds*, where the landscape is noticeably empty except for the beer bottle and lighthouse.[05] Ingmar Bergman's *Seventh Seal* (1957) and *Faro Documents* (1967/1969) are films similarly empty of explicit narrative, encouraging a form of existential imaginative exploration.[06] The impact of the film genre lies not only with its ability to convey wordless narrative through image but also through the control of the director and the highly attuned compositions of the cinematographer. The dialogue and systematic partnership between director and cinematographer is vital in sustaining a dynamic interpretation relationship of complementary skills.

The cinematic work of Christopher Doyle is perhaps the first to have major popular impact through his collaboration with Ang Lee, Wong Kar Wei and Yimou Zhang. The combination of dynamically choreographed camera work and immense focus on the power of physical context creates layers of interpretation that far exceed the simplicity of the story line. Doyle's work creates resonance through the relentless dynamic of the camera's eye.[07] Derek Jarman's photography and film of Dungeness by contrast, suggests an immense power of stillness capturing a different quality of evocation, a sense of isolation, if not desolation. These works primarily engage with space and the power of the land to create an explicit resonance that conveys a depth of meaning that would otherwise be dissipated through words.

The filmic experience is understood through translational control, together with the timing and sequencing of visual imagery. The journey the audience takes through this responsive experience is highly orchestrated, yet film is unable to control the level of interpretive interaction. One of the compelling allures of film is the degree of absence that can be tolerated. The experiential construct of film is obviously different from that of being in space', but there could be an opportunity to examine some of these essential characteristics and consider how these could influence physical language.

LANDSCAPE

Consider a parallel construct that has often been described as of frozen film, found in the physical minimalism of the *'Karasansui'*, or Royal Japanese Stone Gardens[08], where reductive compositions of stone are positioned to create abstracted symbols of folkloric truth or legend. These compositions demand that the audience not only understand the iconography but also experience the vignettes through a prescribed series of compositional frames. The control of the spatial visual framework is, of course, less controlled than that of the filmmaker, as the journey is three dimensional and immersive rather than two dimensional and mono directional. Differences in the physical relationship to object are critical to the way in which the audience comprehends both space and the attendant narrative. While it is complicated to make comparisons between visual genres where the method of construction, constraint, delivery and physical relationship are so different, the fascination lies in the fact that they often share the same intellectual platform. The challenge for the architect is to try to capture nuance that linear drawings and constructed space lack and consider how to explore translational technique. Architectural tools, whether on paper or constructed, have an explicit format - the line, the edge, the boundary, the wall - but the phenomena of fading and conflating a non-linear time sequence are difficult. One must consider levels of dynamic, objects of significance, editorial control and narrative delivery. These must be seen as essential parts of the architectural composition - how do they compare with the techniques of painters and filmmakers?

LANDSCAPE ARCHITECTURE

Burle Marx, Barragan and Noguchi were following in the tradition of those designers who sought inspiration beyond the natural functionality of the ground. Born in Brazil, Burle Marx trained as a painter and botanist producing work that influenced generations. Burle Marx began by challenging the fashion for using Mediterranean plants, preferring those of his native Brazil, and, by observing the natural order of the tropical plant environment, he was able to understand both the hierarchical and parasitical order that allowed vegetation in these latitudes to reach enormous heights. Much of his work was the result of re-introducing the bromeliaceous and saxicole species that could grow in crevices and on granite surfaces and this work, with its sensuous vibrancy and bold heroic geometries, suited the sub-tropical flora of Brazil. His gardens were huge, bold, painterly statements where the concerns were of colour, structure, harmony, volume and expression. These landscapes were a mixture of metaphorical statement and context, often incorporating fragments of local material such as stone, wood and the discarded fragments of old buildings. If one looks at the plans of his gardens, they show clear similarities between the geometric language of constructivist and cubist paintings and some of the formal geometries evident in modernist planning beautifully illustrated in the garden of the house designed by Reno Levi in 1947. These semi- tropical environments were immersive paintings and it took three decades before the work of Burle Marx made an indisputable imprint on architects of the post-modernist period, with groups such as Archigram creating radical scenarios that bore the signs of his influence. Burle Marx was one of the first to understand the significance of the plane and, by placing objects on the surface, he emphasised the plane rather than the object; in doing so, he became perhaps one of the first landscape modernists.

Luis Barragan, a native of Mexico, also used dramatic colour and the sparse materials of his surroundings to create spaces of serenity that recalled the austere nature of his local wild landscape. The constructions he created were of walls, planes, rills, waterspouts, environments of brilliant colour and absolute calm. The landscapes he produced were often surreal, recalling images of De Chirico or Magritte, images of emptiness and desolation.

At a Carnival Ball in Rio; and in the great sweep of the Botafogo gardens that gives human scale to Rio's sublime urban shore. Barragan offered refuge, a quiet space, walled against the assaults of modern civilization: the noise, the crowds, the pollution, the soulless buildings, the telephone. (09)

Japanese American landscape architect Isamu Noguchi echoed aspects of his Japanese ancestry in capturing the essence of myth, reality, performance and theatre. These poetic qualities are deeply embedded in Japanese culture; traces are found in the great gardens of Japan (*Katsura, Ryoan-ji, Daigoji*). The language of these traditional gardens uses minimal material and presents a picture where each formal gesture represents part poetic narrative, where the landscape language is one of metaphor and great subtlety. His education as a sculptor influenced an intuitive inclination to command space through three-dimensional form: there is, of course, an intrinsic paradox in that the sculpture could so easily have become the object in space rather than the space itself.

The forms and materials he used were always part of the architectural palette: stone, timber, concrete, grass, gravel. The open spaces he created used few plants and were, in essence, open rooms. The courtyard garden at CIGNA 1957, designed by Gordon Bunschaft of SOM, is minimal, flat and sculptural, using a restrained palette that completely harmonises with the language of the building. Noguchi worked with Bunschaft again to create the sunken court at the Beinecke Rare Books Library at Yale in 1963. This was a masterly composition in polished marble - inaccessible, yet visible through the glass walls of the library. The sculptural forms created a frozen theatre whose dramatic story can only be created in the mind of the onlooker. The building creates a realm of monastic study and this aura of quiet reflection is brilliantly captured and reflected in its external space. Noguchi was one of the ultimate minimalists, requiring the observer to construct the meaning of each space.

LANDSCAPE URBANISM

Architecture has, with some exceptions, a conservative mantle: where, despite the advances of technology, it rarely challenges the status quo, whereby buildings still have fixed boundaries and a clear definition of internal and external space. The more radical developments in contemporary landscape by designers such as Martha Schwartz, Adriaan Geuze, Claude Cormier, Andrew Cao and Xavier Perrot, have questioned the idea that landscape design needs to be horticultural and the work of this contemporary group presents a challenging model to spatial designers. They confidently appropriate materials used in other forms of production, whether it is concrete, rubber or crystals, to create dramatic installations that question the omnipresence of horticulture. It is within this arena that the worlds of landscape design, sculpture, architecture and narrative overlap. Examples of their work - Central Garden at Gifu (2001)[10], *Schouwburgplein* (1996) by Adriaan Geuze of West 8[11], *The Blue Stick Garde*n (2000) by Cormier (2010), *Cloud Terrace* (2012) by Cao and Perrot - challenge the central precept that gardens must exhort the virtues of nature.

Some of the most important commentary and theoretical perspectives on landscape followed Charles Waldheim's *Symposium on Landscape Urbanism*.[12] This event and subsequent publication was to recognise many of the significant academic positions that existed. While this essay does not attempt to probe the depths of this extensive polemic, the central critique is of some relevance in this context as the issues focus on the failure of urbanists, both designers and policy-makers, to create a city environment that satisfies the needs of the populace. It is argued that the mechanics of creating the city are regimented and rigid, conceived and constructed in a linear manner. The institutionalised nature of the profession supports unitary positions and therefore the argument for disciplinary interaction is clearly articulated. The complex model of an ecological dynamic is hypothecated and the established rule system was challenged. The arguments are many and varied and only limited observations are relevant in this context.

SCALE

James Corner's essay '*Terra Fluxus*' argues that landscape urbanism is the understanding of horizontal surface', conceiving of surfaces, whether synthetic or natural, as indistinguishable and with an almost infinite capacity to store information. The description alludes to an almost archaeological quality, where surfaces are not only read as a physical construct but are also able to show the 'trajectories of shifting demographics'. The ground surface is described as a staging ground 'for both uncertainty and promise' and he continues to acknowledge the imagination as a critical component without which none of the processes or principles can be achieved.[13] The land is unique in being able to adapt almost infinitely to temporal change and it is both its abundant characteristics and ability to mutate that offer the possibility of some sort of interaction through design.

In her essay '*Constructed Ground*', Linda Pollack identifies size as a critical component of how we understand the ground, yet in contrast to popular discourse where the land is commonly presented as strategically scaled, or described in terms of what she calls 'bigness', smaller incidents can be equally important. She maintains that the tradition of the figured ground diagram perpetuates the role of external space being of negligible value, where it is understood as merely space between buildings. '*Yet to build landscape you have to see it, and the ability to do so continues to permeate design culture*'.[14]

The commentary about scale also relates to the human condition, and one might consider land to have a 'vastness' that offers a relationship to terrain and 'smallness' that engages the individual. Pollack maintains that 'scale is an issue inherent in all urban landscapes and is barely addressed in design theory or practice'.[15] There are implicit established relationships (those between the architect and the site, the planners and urban area, the landscape architect and the garden) that acknowledge the scale differences of the components of urban landscape, yet a tradition exists within the professions where each group remains cordoned together with their own fixed boundaries of scale.

These scales need not be fixed: the hierarchies are simply a product of cultural practice. The strategies of professional disconnection produce sterility, and therefore one must ask whether an analytical understanding of scalar language and a subsequent attempt at translation could be a tactic to enrich spatial propositions. The field, the road, the path and the room might have an interchangeability that could alter our strict notational and physical demarcation. If scale were to be altered, or at least cross understood, both detail and function could have a fluidity and boundlessness that is normally difficult to achieve. Perhaps one of the most successful examples is Alvaro Siza's *Leca de Palmeira Pool* (1961), which engages at the scale of the human body, the landscape, the sea and the horizon, 'the project intensifies existing forces by weaving different scales of activity into an existing site'.[16]

TIME

Yet the concept of ground scale has relative values as divisions of space have different geographic tempi; the undulating hills of Europe represent no more than a mound in the context of the major continents. Scale and space are not only a visual construct but also a component of time. To travel through the vast terrain of desert or prairie landscape involves duration and almost indiscernible changes of feature; topographic incidents in these landscapes bear no relation to human scale and the incidents are mere scratches. It is in this context that the rule of measure begins to change and the description of A to B is not by length but duration. Our value system becomes one that is much closer to the experiential and less associated with the measurable. One might therefore consider the notion of space, particularly 'largeness', as both quantifiably visual and also experientially understood. Time is a dimension that is rarely integrated into design thinking as traditionally the architectural model is a unified static idea.

The language of the land demonstrates that not only are the events important but also their relationship to each other. When one considers how the process of translation might occur, it becomes important that the lexicographers identify the building block. To describe and reflect on the quality of each element brings the process of translation nearer.

Conceptually connected to the land, the relationships have often been oblique and associational. Part of this lexicon is literal in that it describes absolute physicality, yet the description is subjective rather than objective. Other characteristics are less tangible and attempt to evoke character. There is no syntactical analysis; more an understanding of phenomena or character that will emerge through the ebb and flow of conversation, but the examples here can be used as references and springboard for ideas.

It is important to state that most of this essay relates to the ideas exchanged with others and through the process of reflection, development and iteration, has bypassed forensic examination. The process of design is not the same as scientific research and production in that it uses an intellectual process in a much more lateral way, interweaving fact, fiction, association and deep knowledge in a way that is difficult to untangle.

The function of the map and the plan is to impose systems of order and consistency, and to convey anything more experiential or nuanced is too complex to execute. These systems of communication lack subtlety and cultural reference and are incapable of describing the types and nature of activity within a building in a particular location.

As this form of synoptic representation has evolved historically, one could assume that the limitation of expression might undermine both breadth of imagination and original thinking. Analytically synoptic representation simply does not have the ability to project nuance. In order to convey the qualities of light, sound, silence, shadow or wind, the line drawing would fail, and a part of the exploration has been to search for other methods of representation. The relentless logic of rectilinear geometry should be challenged by the dendritic geometry of nature.

Notes

(01) Treib, Marc. City Park Rotterdam. In The Public Garden: The Enclosure and Disclosure of the Public Garden, 2002. Rotterdam: NAi Publishers and Architecture International.
(02) Mignot, Dorine, and Eleanor Heartney, eds. Gary Hill. Amsterdam: Stedelijk Museum, 1993.
(03) Wikipedia contributors. "Gary Hill." Wikipedia, The Free Encyclopedia. Last modified June 2013. https://en.wikipedia.org/wiki/Gary_Hill. (Accessed July 2013.)
(04) Elena, Alberto. The Cinema of Abbas Kiarostami. London: Saqi Books, 2005.
(05) Ritchie, Donald. Ozu: Floating Weeds (1959). Berkeley: University of California Press, 1977.
(06) Bragg, Melvyn. The Seventh Seal. London: BFI Publishing, 1998.
(07) Doyle, Christopher. R34 G38 B25: Images by Christopher Doyle. London: Systems Design Limited, 2003.
(08) Young, David, and Michiko Young. The Art of the Japanese Garden. North Clarendon, VT: Tuttle Publishing, 2005.
(09) Walker, Peter, and Melanie Simo. The Legacy of Landscape Architecture: Art or Social Service? Cambridge, MA: MIT Press, 1999.
(10) Richardson, Tim. The Vanguard Landscapes and Gardens of Martha Schwartz. London: Thames & Hudson, 2004.
(11) Loosma, Bart. Superdutch: New Architecture in the Netherlands. New York: Princeton Architectural Press, 2000.
(12) Waldheim, Charles, ed. The Landscape Urbanism Reader. Princeton, NJ: Princeton Architectural Press, 2006.
(13) Corner, James. "Terra Fluxus." In The Landscape Urbanism Reader, edited by Charles Waldheim, 21–33. Princeton, NJ: Princeton Architectural Press, 2006.
(14) Pollak, Linda. "Constructed Ground: Questions of Scale." In The Landscape Urbanism Reader, edited by Charles Waldheim, 127–139. Princeton, NJ: Princeton Architectural Press, 2006.
(15) Pollak, "Constructed Ground"
(16) Pollak, "Constructed Ground"

01
PLOTTING

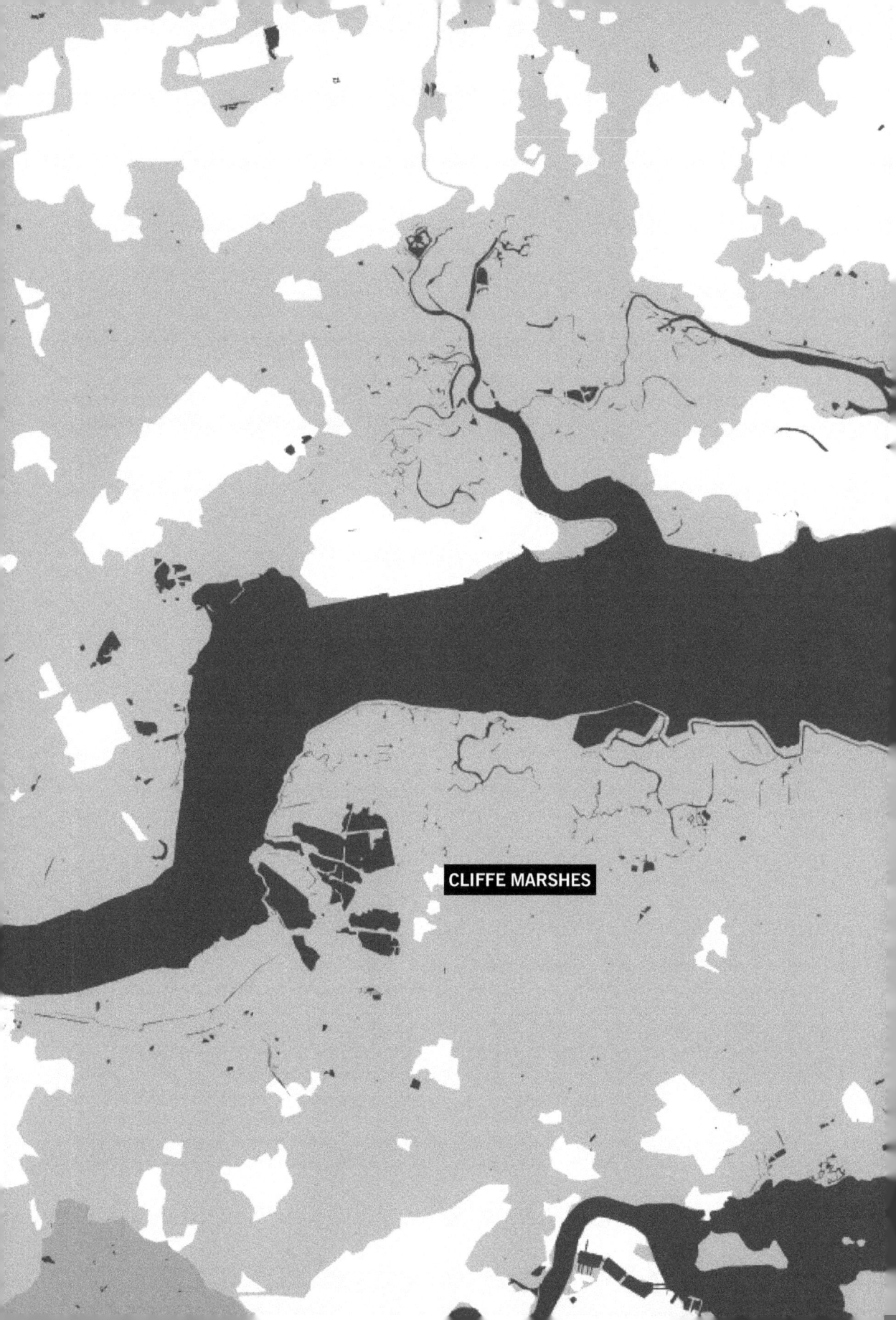

ON PLOTTING

PAOLO ZAIDE & TOM BUDD

The Thames Estuary was home to a number of Plotland developments, informal settlements that sprang up during the early 20th century as city dwellers sought escape from the crowded conditions of London. These plots of land, often sold cheaply and with little regulation, attracted working-class families who built weekend retreats, holiday cottages and, in many cases, permanent homes. The Estuary's proximity to the capital, combined with its open space and sea air, made it an ideal location for these do-it-yourself communities.

On the ground, the Plotlands were a patchwork of self-built bungalows, garden sheds, and converted railway carriages, reflecting the creativity and resilience of their inhabitants. Without formal infrastructure or planning, residents relied on their own labour and resourcefulness to create homes and small communities, many of which would later be absorbed into larger urban developments. These settlements offer a glimpse into a grassroots movement for land, leisure, and independence on the edge of the Thames.

Along this fluid edge of the estuary how do you start plotting? In contemporary landscape urbanism, few concepts carry as much generative weight as plotting. While the term might seem mundane, suggesting the simple act of drawing lines on a map, in the work of James Corner, it is reframed as something far more inventive and vital. Plotting is not merely a technical act of representation; it's a dynamic, creative process that orchestrates spatial relationships, narratives and forces into a provisional choreography. It embraces the complexity and flux of urban ecologies, acknowledging that landscapes are not static objects but ongoing, evolving performances. To understand plotting is to reconsider the designer's role: no longer an authoritative creator imposing fixed form, but a composer of conditions, a facilitator of emergence. It is a design practice that acknowledges uncertainty and multiplicity, offering a methodology better suited for the ecological and social challenges of our time.

Traditional planning and design models often operate under the assumption of control and finality. Masterplans and blueprints offer a vision that, once realized, is a fixed outcome. In contrast, Corner's notion of plotting refuses such closure. It positions design as an ongoing act of composition—one that draws from and reconfigures multiple layers of information, history, ecology, and infrastructure.

Plotting is, in essence, an act of invention. It extracts fragments from a site's cultural and natural systems and recombines them into new spatial narratives. This process is less about drawing a final line and more about scripting possibilities—a kind of design storytelling open to adaptation and reinterpretation. Where traditional cartography seeks to represent reality, plotting in this sense seeks to generate potential. It creates a provisional framework that invites intervention, dialogue, and change. The landscape, in turn, becomes a living text, continuously rewritten by natural forces, human activity, and shifting conditions.

ACROSS SCALES: EXPLORING, INTERPRETING GROUND

Interrogating these landscapes requires methods that adapt across scales of both distance and time. The unique context of the Thames Estuary directly informed the methods employed by the studio to plot and understand these spatial complexities.

Walks: Each year the studio began by slowing down and exploring these sites at a walking pace. In contrast to a top down approach, this act of 'ground up' exploration at a human level allowed for a more delicate understanding of these landscapes, revealing hidden fragments, material qualities and the delicate tapestries of natural, urban and industrial spaces.

Tools: Drawing on landscape operations, (surveying, dissecting, extracting from the ground) the studio employs a variety of tools to catalogue these landscapes. Utilising photography, digital scanning, on-site plotting, AI manipulations, collage and film making, details can be extracted and recomposed to begin to uncover new understandings of the sites. This toolkit combines both digital and physical modes of capture and is constantly being developed as new technologies emerge.

Mapping: The landscapes of the estuary are constantly changing as ever increasing tides wash against dislocated fragments of history. From the studio's initial catalogues there follows a process of layering, mapping and recomposition, tracing fragments through history and using observations to begin to speculate on their potential futures. This in combination with predictive models documenting climate and environmental change forms a unique contextual foundation for the resulting propositions presented by the studio.

The act of *plotting* reveals new worlds within both past and present, creating new ground from the often unseen conditions embedded in place. By uncovering the forces that shape a site—climate, history, local narratives, policy, politics, regulation, and spatial frameworks—it becomes possible to understand the territorial, political, and psychological processes at play. These interactions now matter more than the formal arrangement of space.

Plotting methods offer two complementary vantage points for describing the estuary and its surrounding landscape. While mapping provides a measured, quantifiable representation of data, walks and surveys enable a more personal, qualitative reading of the sites. As exploratory and interpretative tools, these approaches establish the insights necessary to plan and propose architectural design interventions along the estuary.

FORT FOLLOWS FUNCTION

GREG BROOKHOUSE

'The fortification is a special construction, one does not live there, one executes particular actions there, at a particular moment during a conflict....All construction conditions for a building are disrupted by the artifice of war....The establishment of citadels throughout the ages was the result...of an evolution in the value of position...and the invention of new modes of combat.' (01)

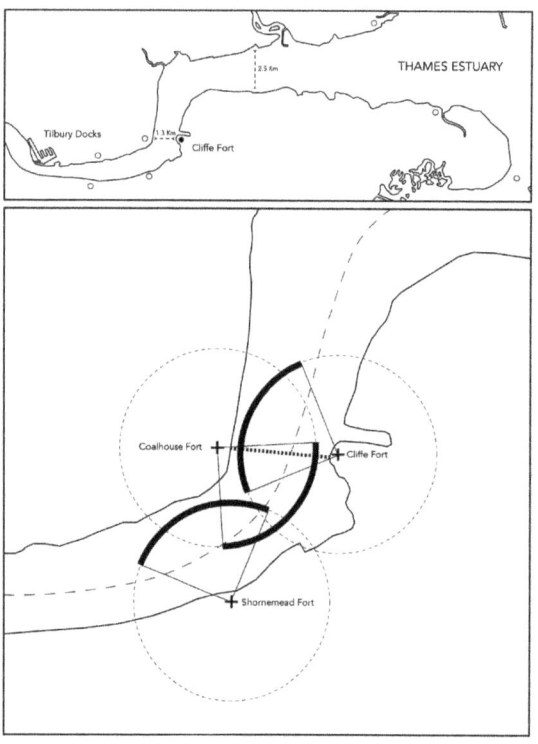

Above: Map of the Thames Estuary, Cliffe Fort and Tilbury
Below: Map of Cliffe, Shornemead and Coalhouse Fort range of fire protecting the narrowing of the Thames

Cliffe Fort stands on low-lying salt flats along the south bank of the Thames, on the Hoo Peninsula in North Kent. Built in the 1860s as part of a campaign to strengthen Britain's defences with a network of coastal forts it has been abandoned since the Second World War. During its life it has been adapted and changed many times in response to different threats and the significant changes in the technology of warfare: initially from the sea and later from the air.

This study investigates how the form of Cliffe Fort and its surrounding landscape were shaped by its strategic purpose and the functions required to fulfil that role with the technology of the time, 'a form conditioned by the circumstances of its production.'(02) More broadly, the Thames Estuary is not a natural landscape but one defined by environmental systems, infrastructure, and social frameworks. Territory here involves systems of power and control shaped by cultural, political, and military forces, where boundaries are established, negotiated, and imposed. The study thus explores how the interaction of natural and man-made systems, alongside these negotiations and impositions, has produced the forts and their distinctive presence in the landscape.

This essay examines these forts through three interconnected perspectives outlined by French theorist and urbanist Paul Virilio. First, bunkers as signs of power: they are symbols of political and military authority, asserting control over both land and psyche, marking territory, and acting as mnemonic devices of potential conflict. This aligns with James Corner's concept of territory as a socially constructed space shaped by systems of power, control, and use, rather than a static physical area.

Second, technological change shapes the landscape: the design and placement of bunkers reflect advances in warfare, from weapons to radar, and as technology evolves, so do their form and function, revealing shifting military strategies over time. Virilio's notion of *dromology*, the logic of speed, emphasizes how the accelerating pace of technology transforms spatial experience, anticipating changes in both strategy and landscape.

Third, negative architecture and framed vision: Virilio describes bunkers as forms of *"negative architecture,"* built to resist the environment. They channel sight to militarily strategic directions, converting the surrounding landscape into a controlled field of operation rather than an open or scenic space, echoing Stuart Elden's concept of territory as comprised of boundaries, zones, and uses produced through negotiation or imposition.

Taken together, these perspectives show how Cliffe Fort encodes a worldview, shaping the Thames Estuary not merely as land but as a dynamic, politically, and technologically mediated territory.

Virilio describes military architecture as engaged

in a race against the accelerating speed of technological change, one it can never fully win: *'Speed has always been the advantage and privilege of the hunter and the warrior'*.[03] Warfare moved from land and sea to the air, and from the outset, Cliffe Fort had to adapt to the increasing speed and power of ships, weapons and, later aircraft. This constant adaptation produced a palimpsest of interventions, from guns housed deep within the fort to rooftop platforms for weapons and observation. The fort also served as a demonstration of Britain's global strength, part of a vast coastal infrastructure protecting interests from Ireland to Hong Kong. Its scale and visibility made it a symbol of economic and military power, echoing other monumental projects like the Atlantic Wall or Cold War nuclear deterrents, where the symbolic assertion of technological supremacy often outweighed purely functional considerations.

Lastly, it is relevant to consider the remaining value of the fort. What is its function when its original purpose, brief and function ceases? The fort has spent longer as a redundant object than a functional instrument of war. This also has parallels with the Atlantic Wall and Virilio's work informs how to understand and value these redundant structures.

Through Virilio's lens, the Thames Estuary emerges as shifting territory, boundaries, zones and uses, formed by negotiation or imposition. Once a militarised corridor to London, Cliffe now embodies obsolescence, preservation, and leisure, signalling both regional decline and new interpretations. This essay uses historical research, drawings as conceptual framing, and photographs as phenomenological documentation to trace how defence transforms into memory, and how military architecture becomes an archive of speed, power, and exclusion.

THAMES TERRITORY AND DEFENCE STRATEGY

Cliffe Fort is one of the 'Palmerston Forts' built after Lord Palmerston's campaign to strengthen Britain's defences against the perceived threat from France during the mid-nineteenth century. Following Britain's victory in the Napoleonic Wars, France rebuilt its navy and expanded its dockyard at Cherbourg, rearming with 'ironclad ships'. Though Britain and France had fought as allies in the Crimean War, French power was still viewed with suspicion. The so-called "three panics" of the 1840s–1850s summed up the climate of strategic reassessment, public anxiety, and political lobbying that led to the *Royal Commission on the Defences of the United Kingdom* (1860).[04]

The Commission's report recommended major works to protect Britain's naval and commercial lifelines. Nowhere was this more urgent than the Thames, gateway to London's docks, naval shipyards, and the Woolwich Arsenal. London's vulnerability to attack via the river was seen as a direct threat to British trade and security.[05] The 1860 scheme proposed new and rebuilt forts at Coalhouse, Shornemead, and Cliffe, together forming a crossfire barrier that could close the Thames against enemy warships. Cliffe's position opposite Coalhouse was key: its guns triangulated fire across the deep-water channel, while a floating boom and minefields could seal the passage entirely. *'The basic characteristic of military architecture has always been…its adaptability to changes in technology and the consequent changes in military tactics and strategy. The result has been a process of constant evolution.'*[06]

The ruins of Cliffe Fort embody what Paul Virilio describes as the essence of military architecture: its ability to reshape perception, movement, and territory. Unlike civic buildings that open outwards, the fort closes itself off. Its façade to the Thames is buried beneath an earth glacis, designed to be invisible to hostile fire. Its parade ground is ringed with banks that shield support areas from shells. To approach the fort is to encounter what Virilio calls a "controlled visual field": openness restricted, horizons compressed, and vision reduced to what the military deems strategically useful.

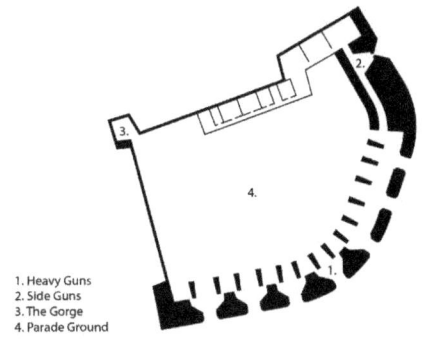

1. Heavy Guns
2. Side Guns
3. The Gorge
4. Parade Ground

Four functional zones of the fort determined by the cannon technology of the period

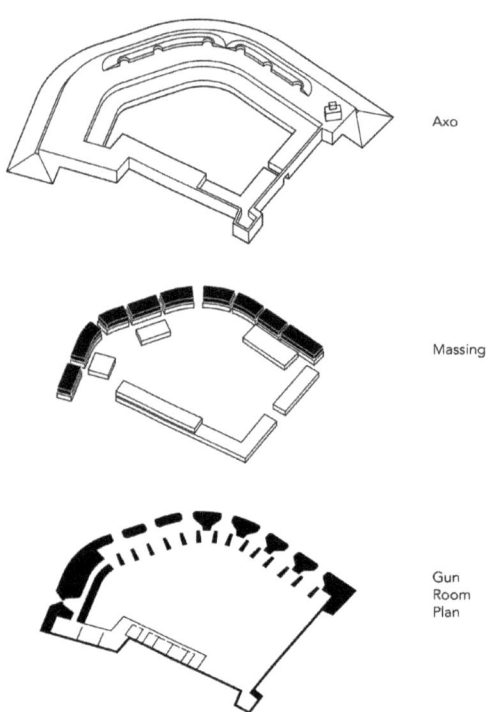

Retrofitted service corridors with glazed observation panels enabled safe, isolated lighting of ammunition bays, reducing ignition hazards

This corresponds to what might be termed a "negative architecture." Rather than being defined by what it presents, the fort is defined by what it excludes. It subtracts visibility, accessibility, and openness from the landscape. Much of its structure is hidden or deliberately obscured, and its function is difficult to read once the guns and tactical installations have been removed. Even at the height of its operational life, much of Cliffe's military effectiveness depended not on what could be seen, but on what was denied: unseen trajectories of fire, invisible underwater obstructions, and the silent reach of heavy ordnance.

The Thames landscape, therefore, becomes both framed and excluded. What is framed is narrow and instrumental: the navigable channel, the arcs of fire across its surface, and the strategic routes leading upstream to London. What is excluded is everything beyond this militarised gaze settlement, marshland, labour, and the ordinary uses of the river. In this way, Cliffe Fort not only defended the nation but redefined the very way the Thames was perceived: not as a working landscape of commerce and community, but as a potential battlefield seen through the narrowed aperture of military vision.

HISTORY OF DESIGN INFLUENCES

The three forts drew on lessons from the Crimean and American Civil Wars, when rapid advances in naval technology reshaped the spatial and temporal dynamics of warfare. Mid-nineteenth-century combat introduced manoeuvrable, iron steam-powered ships whose speed and firepower compressed defensive response times and redefined strategic space. Russian forts at Sebastopol and Kronstadt, with curved walls, tiered casemates, and even underwater mines, impressed the Royal Navy with their ability to control approaches and resist bombardment. Fort Sumter's stand against iron ships in 1863 confirmed that such designs could withstand both naval and land attack. Over the same period, rifled artillery replaced smooth-bore cannons, extending range and accuracy, further accelerating the cadence of battle.

This reflected Paul Virilio's concept of *Dromology*: how speed transforms our experience of space and time. The steamship's velocity compressed the time available for defensive reaction, while rifled guns stretched the reach of fire across landscapes once considered secure. Forts like Cliffe were forced to adapt, becoming architectures of delay, designed not for monumental endurance but to manage fleeting moments of encounter. In this sense, technological change left its mark not only on military strategy but on the built form of defence itself, embedding the acceleration of modern warfare into the very geometry of walls, fields of fire, and the narrowed apertures of vision.'The evolution of military architecture is moulded by the weapons used against it and by those used in support [...] Throughout history there was a continual swing in the balance of superiority of attack and defence.'[07]

The final design of Cliffe Fort, completed in 1875, was dictated by contemporary cannon technology and organised into four functional zones. Facing the Thames, the main guns sat in granite-faced bombproof casemates, their walls angled to deflect shells and fitted with rails for manual aiming; later, rope curtains were added for crew protection. Upstream, lighter guns defended a river minefield from an open terrace, both gun zones underpinned by a massive concrete slab and served by basement armouries with shell lifts. The gorge contained accommodation and defensive towers with rifle loopholes, while the central parade ground linked all areas and provided access to stores. Supplies arrived by river, tramway or a military road to Shornemead. Late-stage alterations reduced the number of guns but increased their power. Some casemates being filled with concrete for extra strength. A hazardous reliance on oil and candle lighting in the ammunition stores prompted the addition of separate service corridors with glazed windows for safer illumination.

One of Cliffe Fort's original 1860 Commission roles

was to guard a Thames minefield, initially a floating boom between Coalhouse and Cliffe, later replaced by electrically operated mines controlled from the fort, a shift influenced by American Civil War innovations. This required roof-mounted searchlights and quick-firing guns to scan for enemy boats, while a sloping earth glacis shielded and concealed the casemates, forming a protective ditch with access to the mines. Yet by its 1875 completion, advances in gunnery rendered Cliffe obsolete as a battery, with Coalhouse alone able to cover the channel. The Franco-Prussian War, the 1904 *Entente Cordiale*, and the rise of Germany further diminished its strategic purpose. By the 1880s, torpedo boats, breech-loaded naval guns, and new tactics prompted calls to replace the Thames forts with modern low-profile batteries; instead, Cliffe's casemates were strengthened with cast iron and concrete, gun numbers reduced, and the glacis extended. The roof became the main weapons platform, fitted with lighter quick-firing guns to protect the minefield from fast, agile attackers.

In the 1880s, Cliffe Fort's strategic position on the Thames saw it become one of only five UK bases to operate the *Brennan* torpedo, the first operational, wire-guided underwater missile, capable of striking ships at depths up to 2,000 metres away with precision. Powered by twin cable drums driven by a stationary steam engine, it used gyroscopes for stability, a secret depth-control mechanism, and a shielded night light for targeting. Operating it required major alterations: western casemates and ammunition stores were converted into an engine room, a new underground torpedo store was built, and a long sloping slipway extended into the river for launch. Control demanded height, so a hydraulically powered capsule on a telescopic piston was built to rise through the open battery roof, allowing the operator to steer via electrical signals to the engine room. Though the capsule and lift are gone, the circular sloping concrete roof apron, shaft opening, and remnants of the steel lift shaft remain as unique traces of this innovative defence.

The 1905 *Owen Committee Report*, marked "Secret," reviewed Britain's 1860s–70s coastal defences and recommended downgrading many Palmerston Forts, including Cliffe. Assuming continued maritime supremacy and the navy's ability to quickly intercept enemy fleets, it argued fixed defences should merely threaten enough damage to force the enemy to fight at a disadvantage, rather than withstand prolonged siege. With attacking ships needing to navigate miles of pilotage waters and pass under the heavy guns of Sheerness before reaching the Thames' commercial shipping, an assault was deemed "practically non-existent" under modern conditions. The report hastened Cliffe Fort's decline: the Brennan torpedo was removed in 1906, the fort disarmed and mothballed, its role made obsolete by the navy's dominance and evolving naval warfare.

During the First World War, Cliffe Fort's role was revived as a gatekeeper for the Thames, maintaining a rebuilt minefield and floating boom between Coalhouse and Cliffe. New searchlights, guns, and a two-storey rooftop watch post were added, while the gorge housed soldiers and adapted married quarters. Yet most of the fort lay redundant: casemates and ammunition stores were empty, the glacis overgrown, and only the *Brennan* torpedo's lift shaft remained. As the naval threat waned, a new danger emerged from the air, German Zeppelin raids, prompting further adaptations for anti-aircraft guns, aerial searchlights, and an observation station, even as the fort's obsolescence deepened.

After the First World War, Cliffe Fort was effectively mothballed, used only for occasional training, with most guns removed. By 1927 only two remained. In the late 1930s it was sold to the Alpha Cement Company, which added a jetty and tramway to transport dredged sand and gravel. During the Second World War, the fort was again requisitioned as a gatekeeper for the Thames, with new guns and searchlights installed and an additional floor added to the northern watchtower, though much of its wartime use remains unclear.

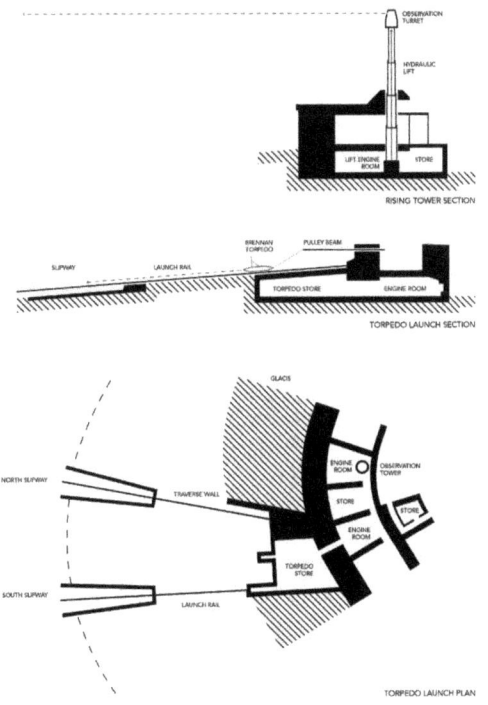

Cliffe Fort became one of five UK bases for the Brennan torpedo in the 1880s — the first operational wire-guided underwater missile.

1945 TO THE PRESENT DAY

The fort was returned to Alpha Cement in 1945. Since then, it has stood derelict, briefly housing the company's sailing club in the 1960s before neglect and quarrying altered its condition. Changes in the water table flooded the basement and parade ground, while vandalism stripped it. In 1971, it became a Scheduled Monument, yet it remains on Historic England's "at risk" register, part of what Marcus Binney calls "Britain's vanishing heritage."[08]

Our interpretation of such military architecture is ambivalent. Its functional clarity is lost, its weapons gone, yet the ruin endures. Layers of adaptation and decay now form what might be read as a physical geology of conflict, technology, and abandonment. As Pepper and Hall note, nowhere else in architectural history does the demand for firmness feel so absolute, while the link to beauty appears so tenuous.[09] Cliffe embodies what Virilio described as an "archaeology of the brutal encounter": its dark vaults, flooded casemates, and parasitic growths now evoke the haunting atmosphere of Piranesi's *Carceri*.[10]

The comparison with Virilio's study of the Atlantic Wall is instructive. Like the German bunkers, Cliffe has outlived its tactical role to acquire new symbolic force. Virilio's 'anthropomorphic' reading of the bunker, its apertures like blind eyes, its bulk like a mute sentinel, applies here too. Once an instrument of power, it is now a blank monument, its original gaze closed off for decades.

Today, the fort's meaning is reshaped through competing uses. Heritage groups campaign for preservation, while explorers and "urban archaeologists" create alternative narratives through digital media, celebrating danger, decay, and inaccessibility. In this, Cliffe has been transformed: from military infrastructure designed to exclude, to a terrain of leisure and spectacle designed to attract, even if through risk and ruin.

This dramatic change in function raises broader questions of territory and power. For Virilio, territory is always composed of boundaries, zones, and uses, products of negotiation or imposition. Cliffe once imposed absolute control over the Thames, fixing its meaning as a military corridor. Today, its value is negotiated: between heritage discourse, subcultural exploration, and regional decline. The shift from war machine to leisure landscape does not erase its violent origins but reframes them. Its obsolescence signals more than decay; it reveals how changing worldviews reorder space, how the architecture of defence becomes the archaeology of memory, and how Cliffe Fort continues to embody power, though now as an ambivalent monument rather than an active shield.

Notes

(01) Paul Virilio, *Bunker Archaeology* (Princeton: Princeton Architectural Press, 1976), 42.
(02) V. Watson, in J. Madge, Sabbioneta Cryptic City (Biblioteque McLean, 2011), 5.
(03) Virilio, Bunker Archeology, p.19
(04) A. Williams and S. Newsome, *Cliffe Fort Hoo Peninsula Medway Kent*, Historic England, 2011, vol. 2, 219, www.historicengland.org.uk.
(05) "Coast Defences: Description and Purpose." *Victorian Forts and Artillery*. Accessed December 21, 2021. http://www.victorianforts.co.uk
(06) K. Mallory and A. Ottar, *Architecture of Aggression* (London: Architectural Press, 1973), 269. "Coast defences: description and purpose," Victorian Forts, accessed 21 December 2021, www.victorianforts.co.uk.
(07) Hughes, Q. *Military Architecture*. British Library Cataloguing in Publication Data, 1974.
(08) Save Britain's Heritage, *Deserted Bastions* (Save Britain's Heritage, 1993), introduction by Binney M., 1.
(09) S. Pepper and N. Adams, Firearms and Fortifications (Chicago: University of Chicago Press, 1986)
(10) Virilio, Bunker Archeology, p.19

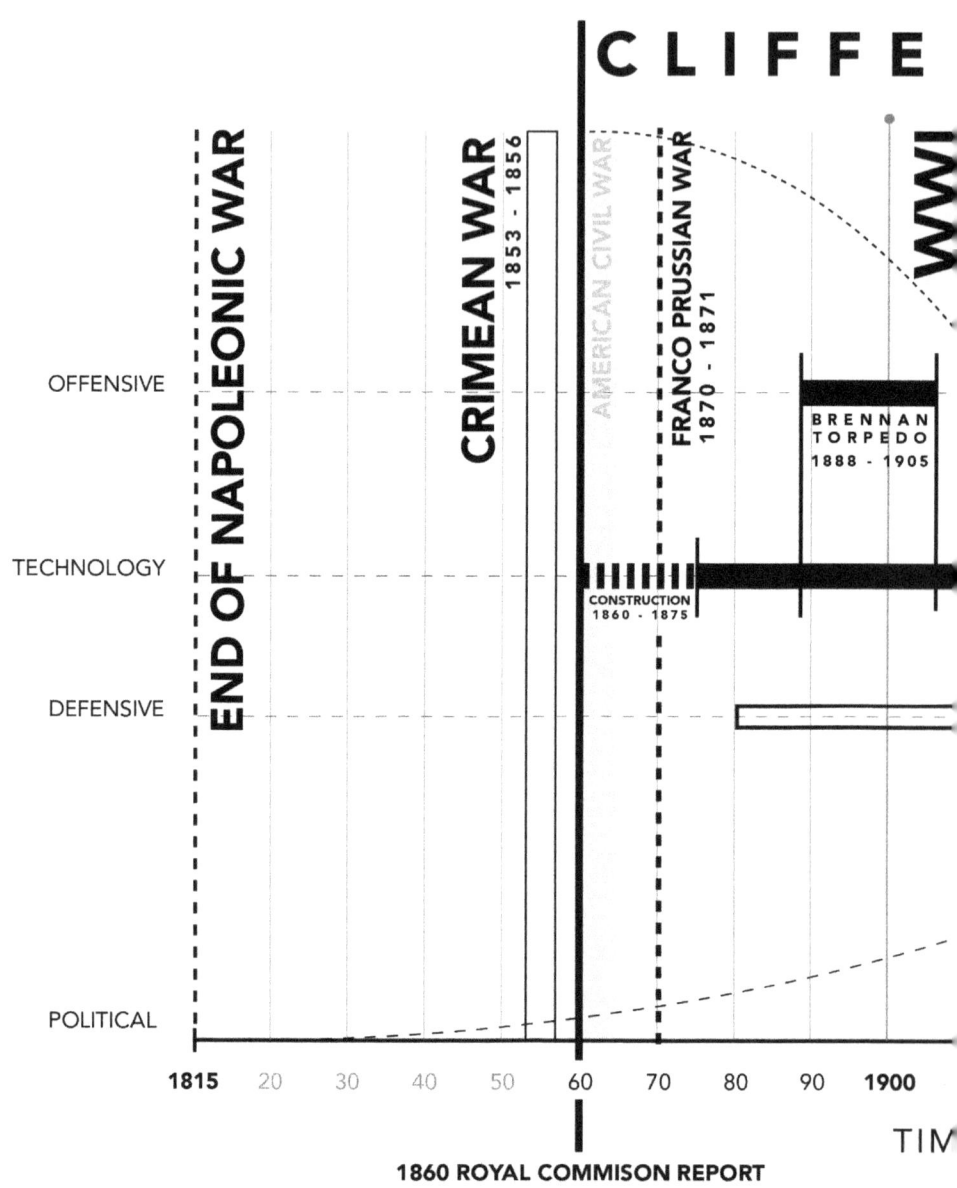

Above
Timeline of Cliffe Fort's development and decline, mapped against major political milestones and advancements in military technology

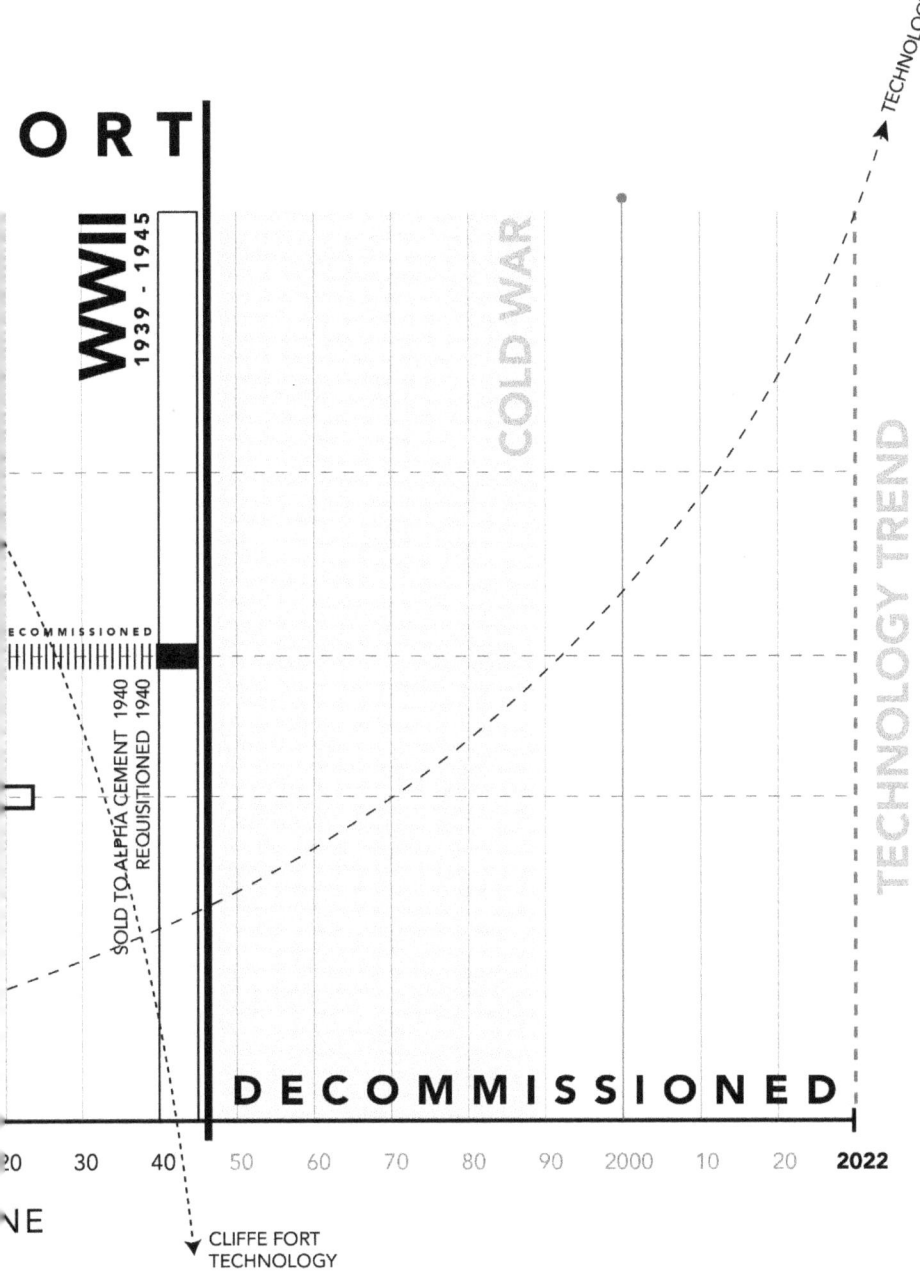

SACRIFICIAL PLOTS

REECE MURRAY

Sacrificial sites—spaces designed to absorb and mimic destruction—occupy a unique role in shaping landscapes both materially and imaginatively. On the Hoo Peninsula, such sites reveal how military deception, police training infrastructures, and controlled architectural decay function as deliberate acts of spatial manipulation. These zones are examined in terms of their military origins and their subsequent transformation through cultural narratives and ecological processes.

Structured in four parts, this essay first describes decoys created in the landscape, then examines their historical role as *simulations* designed to avert real threats, before considering their afterlife as *simulacra* in film and staged scenarios, and finally their transformation into ecological and cultural terrains.

Building on this, the paper explores how such spaces, once designed for tactical sacrifice, have become fertile ground for cinematic and literary representation. In particular, the decrepit marshes of Charles Dickens' *'Great Expectations'* and the constructed warzone in Stanley Kubrick's *'Full Metal Jacket'*, both engaging with the atmospheric and psychological qualities embedded in sacrificial landscapes. These works underscore the terrain's ability to conjure dread, isolation and ambiguity. Through the theoretical frameworks of *simulations* and *simulacra*, I examine how military and cinematic strategies can overlap with an aim to create intense, ephemeral atmospheres. Ultimately, this broadens the idea of sacrifice to include not only physical destruction but also the transformative, narrative potential of these landscapes in the cultural and ecological senses.

The Hoo Peninsula, once a site of high military strategic value, today carries a quieter but no less resonant purpose. Though its bunkers, training ranges and decoy architecture appear neglected, these remnants are not nothing. They have become active agents in the cultural reimagining of British landscapes. The terrain, marked by its bleak marshes and overgrown ruins, has served as an ideal location for symbolic narratives in literature and film.

Charles Dickens, born in Portsmouth yet familiar with the Kentish terrain, drew on this geography in his portrayal of Pip's terrifying encounter with Magwitch in *Great Expectations*. The opening scene, in which a boy is alone in a fog-laden marsh and approached by a threatening stranger, sets the tone for a novel engaged with social guilt, fear, and transformation. The dark, foreboding atmosphere, shaped by marshes and their ominous sounds, places the reader within a sacrificial landscape shaped equally by historical reality and literary imagination.

Similarly, Stanley Kubrick's *Full Metal Jacket* reappropriates British terrain as a surrogate for Vietnam. Scenes filmed at Cliffe Marshes and nearby estuarial areas mimic parts of Saigon, transforming ruins into simulations of active conflict. The opening scene with its claustrophobic barracks and verbal assault evokes a scene of psychological suffocation. This is not merely a training ground, but a theatre of pressure and submission, mimicking how sacrificial sites function in both real-world and theatrical battle.

HOO PENINSULA ARCHITECTURE AS DECOYS

To classify these 'sacrificial sites', one must first grasp the historical context in which they exist: Hoo Peninsula's military and fortified history.

Military architecture is deeply intertwined with the broader history of architecture. War and resources assigned to such scenarios have acted as enablers for increased development in the urban and rural realms. Many established urban environments originated from military and fortified elements.[01] Ironically, the earliest records of 'sacrificial architecture' can be the most permanent forms, such as castles and forts. The earliest known term for architectural destruction, coined in 1613, was *'slighting'*. This refers to its users deliberately damaging high status buildings to reduce their value as military, administrative or social structures.[02] The relevance of the term serves to establish some of the earliest practices of self-assigned sites of sacrifice. The structures and fortifications are purposely built, only to be intentionally damaged or destroyed. The value of such an act derives from preventing the need for further destruction.

Historical records show that the Hoo Peninsula served as a first line of defence during the two World Wars of the 20th century, demonstrated in the defensive positions located throughout the G.H.Q line (General Headquarters Line) in WW2. The marshy coastline offered natural defensive advantages, though not without limitations, affecting the capabilities of technology. With advancement of warfare, specifically aerial, the Hoo Peninsula had to adapt to the fear of bombardment from the skies. With this came the requirement of protecting cities and airfields from targeted strikes. To counter this, designated targets for deliberate destruction were constructed. In turn, they were sacrificed in due course, to direct the line of fire away from intended targets of the Luftwaffe.[03]

View of Curtis's and Harvey Ltd Explosives Factory, Cliffe 2021

Decoy architecture was conceived for the use of deceptive structures, becoming a more recent form of sacrificial site. The British military classified this phenomenon as a form of intelligence labelled 'strategic deception'. This involved misleading the enemy through false signals, simulated troop movements, and dummy equipment.[04] *'Tactical deception'* is the act itself, with an adversary using ammunition, resources and possibly risking their own life in engagement with the decoy targets.

Such undertakings were led by Colonel John Turner, taking charge of the Air ministry's 'Decoy Program' in 1939. The primary goal was to prevent casualties, mimicking existing airfields, equipment, troops and barracks, which can be seen located in and around Gravesham (illustrated later). The construction and military engineering consisted of temporary structures designed to simulate explosions and fires, misleading enemy targeting, conducted behind the scenes from *'control bunkers'*.

During WWII, Starfish sites were nighttime decoys that used controlled fires to simulate a burning city or industrial area, while QL sites used lighting effects to replicate specific industrial features like factories, marshalling yards, and even vehicle headlights. Both were types of bombing decoys designed to deceive the German Luftwaffe into dropping bombs on relatively uninhabited areas away from their intended targets. These replicated the burning of cities (Starfish sites), towns and villages (QL sites).[05] Two types of false airfield were used, 'Q' sites being used during night raids, and day sites being termed 'K' sites.[06] The use of flammable, lightweight materials for the destructive theatrics contributed to the lack of surviving structures. The 'control bunkers' are the more permanent remnants of these sites today.

In these cases, architecture can be seen as performative, purposefully constructed to serve targeted destruction, and in exchange, mitigating damage and loss from surrounding airfields and cities of higher value.

SIMULATION AND CONSTRUCTED GROUND

Simulation is the process of imitating or recreating the real. In Baudrillard's terms, simulation is not just faking something real, but replacing it, creating a world that functions as if it is real, even though it is not.

Information about these sites remained classified until 1977, when Charles Cruickshank documented them in his book *'Deception in World War II'*, based on newly declassified files.[07]

In total, approximately 797 decoy sites were listed in the United Kingdom, with 1100 types of decoys, including airfields, decoy towns, marshalling yards, steelworks, foundry and factory complexes.[08] By the end of the war, statistics showed that dummy airfields had been bombed 443 times — even more than the actual airfields, which were hit 434 times. Calculations made at the end of WW2 stated 5% of the bombings carried out by German bombers were diverted. "We recognised it as a decoy site only at the last moment, as we were crossing the threshold of a flarepath. Our downward identification light signals eventually got the lights of a real airfield to appear from the blackout!"[09]

In this sense, architecture became a performance: sites were built not to last but to be destroyed, staging destruction to protect more valuable targets. This logic of simulation forms a conceptual bridge to their later role in film, where the same landscapes again function as convincing substitutes for reality. This can be identified by three primary characteristics:

Control
WWII decoy bunkers and the Kent Metropolitan Police Specialist Training Centre (KMPSTC) both demonstrate how control is central to staging deception. Control bunkers coordinated the lighting and fires of QL sites, drawing Luftwaffe bombing raids away from real targets. Today, observation points at training centres serve a similar function: overseeing orchestrated scenarios, turning the training centre itself into both a stage and decoy.

Deception
Psychological persuasion is key. Decoys mimic familiar structures through light and form, convincing adversaries of their authenticity. In WWII, flarepaths and oil fires mimicked burning cities; at KMPSTC, streets and facades imitate London neighbourhoods, immersing officers in lifelike environments. These constructed landscapes function as rehearsal spaces, shaping how participants perceive and respond to threats.

Destruction
Sacrificial sites are designed with destruction in mind. WWII decoys absorbed enemy bombs, while police training grounds simulate riots and urban conflict. Both are built to host repeated cycles of damage and renewal.

In each case, architecture is not static but performative: it is built to be attacked, burned, or demolished. This performance of destruction demonstrates how simulation works across military and civic contexts, bridging wartime deception with contemporary staged training.

SIMULACRA AND CONSTRUCTED FICTION

A simulacrum is a copy or representation of something. But for Baudrillard, it is not just a simple copy, it can become detached from any original reference and take on a life of its own.

Q sites were among the most striking examples of wartime simulacra. Built as decoy airfields, they recreated the lighting and layout of real runways using flarepaths, lamps, and lightweight structures for night-time operations. Operated from concealed bunkers, they lured German bombers into dropping payloads on empty fields rather than actual military targets. These sites were fabrications designed to pass as reality, architecture created only to be destroyed. In Baudrillard's terms, they functioned as early simulacra, representations that no longer referred to an original but operated independently as convincing substitutes. When such landscapes later reappeared in cultural contexts, for instance, Stanley Kubrick's decision to use Cliffe Marshes as a stand-in for Vietnam in *Full Metal Jacket*, they embodied a second layer of simulation: a copy of a copy. The same terrain that once staged destruction as a wartime survival tactic was later re-staged for cinema, producing atmospheres of dread and confinement for audiences far removed from the war itself.

This shared logic between military deception and cinematic staging can be better understood through Baudrillard's theory of simulation and simulacra. Baudrillard's concept suggests that in a postmodern world, representations no longer refer to reality but to other representations. The *Q Sites* of WWII were simulacra by design. They mimicked the look and light of real cities under attack, simulating fires and street lighting to misdirect enemy bombers. When these same sites later became film locations, or influenced fictional depictions of war, they were recycled as simulations of simulations.

In *Full Metal Jacket*, Cliffe Marshes became a cinematic copy of a copy. It stands in for a Vietnamese city, which itself stands for an abstraction of war. The audience is immersed in a film designed to feel authentic, even though every element is curated, controlled and staged. The result is dread and confinement, the violence feels real for the viewer, even though the environment is entirely simulated. Similarly, Dickens' Great Expectations shows how landscapes can act as simulacra. The marshes are not simply settings, but characters themselves, embodying dread, isolation and ambiguity. The fog is not merely weather, but a veil, concealing class barriers, moral ambiguity and danger. Both examples demonstrate how sacrificial sites, once built for tactical sacrifice, have evolved into cultural terrains that generate meaning through atmosphere, narrative and symbolism.

The Metropolitan Police Specialist Training Centre, Gravesend 2021

TODAY'S CONSTRUCTS: THE KMPSTC POTEMKIN VILLAGE

The site constructions consist of an observation point, reminiscent of the control bunkers used on WWII Starfish sites. Both Cliffe Marshes and the Kent Police Specialist Training Centre (KMPSTC) contain mimicked environments: at Cliffe, false flarepaths and oil fires once simulated burning towns, while at KMPSTC hollow façades of pubs, shops, and housing reproduce the fabric of a London street. These sites share an architecture of deception: built for fleeting use, yet persistent in their material remains.

The term *Potemkin village* derives from Prince Grigory Potemkin, who staged grand but superficial villages to impress Catherine the Great in 18th-century Russia.[10] KMPSTC can be understood as a modern Potemkin village: a fabricated townscape constructed to conceal its own artifice beneath familiar details. Officers encounter a place that appears to be a functioning community, yet its purpose is solely to stage controlled scenarios. Like Potemkin's villages, its role is not permanence but performance, where appearance masks reality.

Like the story of Potemkin, KMPSTC's architecture is deliberately fictitious, designed to simulate authenticity while concealing its constructed purpose. It is designed to convince participants of its authenticity while masking its constructed nature. Here, the "tourist" is not Catherine the Great, but the trainee police officer, encountering an environment curated by planners and instructors to produce specific experiences. The architecture directs perception much as wartime decoys once directed enemy bombers

Reliability of the lens in documenting such sites raises further questions. Just as Potemkin villages and, later, WWII decoys were designed to mislead, photographs of KMPSTC can also distort or exaggerate what is seen. Different lenses, altered perspectives, or digital editing can shift how these sites are read, moving them away from documentation toward simulation. As Claire Zimmerman indicates in Photographic Architecture in the Twentieth Century, the photograph no longer indexes the real. It now equalises the real and the imaginary.

This recalls both the example of Cliffe Marshes and the fabricated Arab town *"Chicago"* constructed by the Israeli Defence Force, where photographs blur documentation and fiction. In each case, architecture itself is designed to deceive, and photography extends this deception into new registers of representation. In this way, both wartime decoys and Kent's training grounds operate as Potemkin villages: architectures of concealment and control that blur the truth and performance. Whether experienced directly by participants or mediated through photographs, they are simulated landscapes – staged realities that embody the sacrificial logic of architecture.

Since its invention, photography has often been considered a medium of documentation, but sacrificial sites reveal how images can deceive as much as they record. As Claire Zimmerman indicates in *Photographic Architecture in the Twentieth Century*, the photograph no longer indexes the real. It now equalises the real and the imaginary. In the case of sites like KMPSTC photographed by James Rawlings or Cliffe Marshes, the line between record and fabrication is blurred, a photograph of a hollow façade or ruined bunker can appear authoritative, yet it conceals layers of staging, orchestration, and performance.

Gregory Sailer's photographic project The Potemkin Village exemplifies this slippage. His work captures fabricated training towns such as *"Carson City"* in the United States, designed for military exercises. The resulting images resemble ordinary urban landscapes, yet they depict no actual community. Similarly, Adam Broomberg and Oliver Chanarin's access to the IDF's mock-Arab town *"Chicago"* produced photographs that, through forced perspective and rigid objectivity, mimic the aesthetics of virtual reality rather than documentary truth. These examples resonate with Kent's training ground and wartime decoy sites: each produces an environment that looks authentic but is constructed for controlled performance. Photographs of these sites risk perpetuating the deception by framing façades as full buildings, and training grounds as real towns.

In this sense, photography extends the logic of sacrificial architecture. The sites themselves are designed to deceive in material form, and their images often reinforce or even amplify that deception, making temporary and staged environments appear permanent and real.

TOMORROW'S ECOLOGIES: STAGING THE THAMES ESTUARY'S FUTURE

The Thames Estuary, long a site of exchange, invasion, and industrial activity, is increasingly being understood not as a wasteland, but as a location of layered history. It contains the physical residue of past strategies (defensive trenches, decoy bunkers, bomb craters) and the atmospheric resonance through cinema and literature. This physical layering complicates the narrative. Sacrifice here is not final. Instead, the coastal landscape absorbs and reconfigures its meanings over time. Once a decoy for wartime attacks, it is now a refuge for wildlife. Once a set for urban combat, it is now a set for speculative fiction. The 'sacrificial' is not erased; it is recontextualised.

As Kent's landscape shifts its spatial policies toward conservation and ecological restoration, the estuary's identity must also shift. It is now the UK's second most biodiverse zone, home to thousands of species. The very qualities that made it suitable for military deception, its remoteness, flatness and volatility now make it ideal for nonhuman life. The landscape evolves from a zone of human conflict to a stage of ecological renewal. In re-examining the Hoo Peninsula and Cliffe through overlapping military, cinematic, literary, and ecological lenses, a richer understanding of 'sacrificial sites' emerges. These are not merely locations designed to absorb or deflect destruction. They are terrains of transformation: Sites whose purpose, meaning, and significance have evolved over time.

What began as military decoys or temporary police training stages have become part of the imaginative architecture of cultural memory. Dickens and Kubrick each demonstrate the landscape's power to evoke mood, moral tension, and psychological intensity. Their use of these terrains mirrors the military's own approach to simulation.

The logic of the sacrificial site, then, is not bound to destruction. It is bound to potential. The trenches and bunkers, the fog and fire, the signage and false facades point to a landscape in change. The Thames Estuary does not end with the memory of war, but it begins anew with each representation and adaptation, ecological or otherwise.

Through this filmic and ecological lens, the Hoo Peninsula is no longer seen as a peri-urban backdrop. It becomes a stage that hosts not only the ghosts of past conflicts (through its clandestine elements), but also the aspirations of new futures, seen in its ecological growth. These are not hard defensive structures, but zones of softness, blurring, and transformation. These moments of short-term sacrifice lead to a longer, unknown timeline of ecological growth.

Pillbox bunkers were used for the defense against a possible enemy invasion East Tilbury, Essex

Notes

(01) Laura Pastoreková, Peter Vodrážka "(In)Visible Elements of the City Military Architecture in the Context of Urban Structure Development" Procedia Engineering 161 (2016) 2161 – 2167 (2016) 2166, https://doi.org/10.1016/j.proeng.2016.08.809.
(02) Nevell, Richard (2019), "The archaeology of slighting: a methodological framework for interpreting castledestruction in the Middle Ages", The Archaeological Journal, 177 (1): 99–139
(03) Collin Dobson, Fields of deception : Britain's bombing decoys of World War II. (Methuen Publishing Ltd;Revised ed. edition, 2013) 1.
(04) Collin Dobson, Fields of deception : Britain's bombing decoys of World War II. (Methuen Publishing Ltd; Revised ed. edition, 2013) Preface 1.
(05) Sarah Newsome, Edward Carpenter and Peter Kendall, Hoo Peninsula, Kent: Hoo Peninsula Historic Landscape Project (English Heritage, 2013) 80.
(06) Collin Dobson, Fields of deception : Britain's bombing decoys of World War II. (Methuen Publishing Ltd; Revised ed. edition, 2013) 34.
(07) Cruickshank, Charles. Deception in World War II, (Oxford University Press; First Edition), 1979
(08) Collin Dobson, Fields of deception : Britain's bombing decoys of World War II. (Methuen Publishing Ltd;Revised ed. edition, 2013) Preface 3.
(09) Wallis, Ken, interviews by Huby Fairhead, Decoy Sites, 1996, Foreward
(10) Gregor Sailer, Linde B. Lehtinen, and Walter Moser, The Potemkin Village, Kehrer Verlag; Bilingual edition, 2017, Pg.149

ADAPTIVE GROUND

GREG BROOKHOUSE

As sea levels rise, many villages in North Kent face an increasing risk of flooding and erosion, lacking adequate infrastructure to manage their coastlines. Cliffe stands at the edge of this vulnerability. This project asks: can a more sustainable development model be created—one that strengthens defences while also creating opportunities for communities to benefit from their evolving environment and emerging coastline?

The proposal critiques traditional hard defences that treat coastlines as barriers and instead explores an adaptive typology, informed by the vernacular architecture and landscape cues of North Kent. Rather than viewing defence as solely binary, the project proposes a layered system in which sea walls are seeded with reed beds, research stations, community spaces, plant nurseries, and dwellings. These insertions transform the wall from a line of separation into an inhabitable threshold, enabling a gradient of engagement with the marsh while protecting the village. As the headquarters for the Future Kent Coastline Commission, the project offers a robust, sustainable alternative to aggressive coastal management. By embedding research, community interaction, and environmental stewardship into the structure, the design turns risk into opportunity—where defence infrastructure doubles as shared civic space and ecological laboratory.

The speculative map is set in 2122. The wetland is flooded, and the first five meters of coastline are planted with the reed strategy. This is the goal of the scheme: to plant Kent with a resilient new method that protects it while sacrificing its lowlands to safeguard London from floods and foster regional ecology.

Cliffe village, on the Hoo Peninsula in North Kent, sits at the edge of the marsh, three kilometres from the Thames. With rising waters projected to flood the marsh, Cliffe risks becoming an unprepared settlement on the foreshore. Historically defined by defence, from medieval walls to Victorian fortifications guarding London, the village now faces a different threat of inundation. Its vernacular fabric, with houses over 200 years old, occupies the threshold between settlement and wetland, making it a testing ground for adaptation. Instead of isolating the community behind barriers, the proposal transforms the sea wall into both protection and occupation. Populated with reed beds, research spaces, and community structures, it links ecological renewal with social use, turning risk into resource.

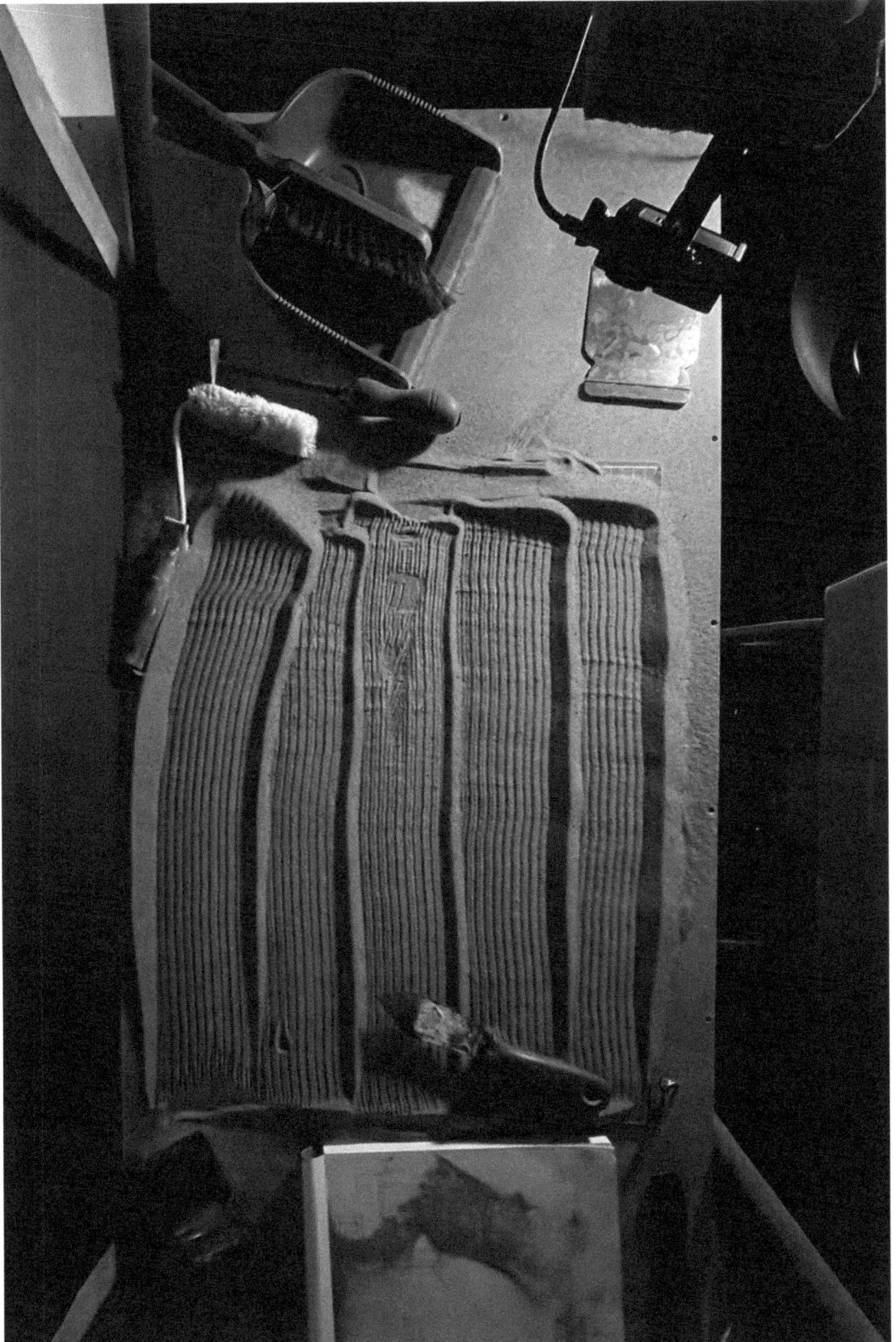

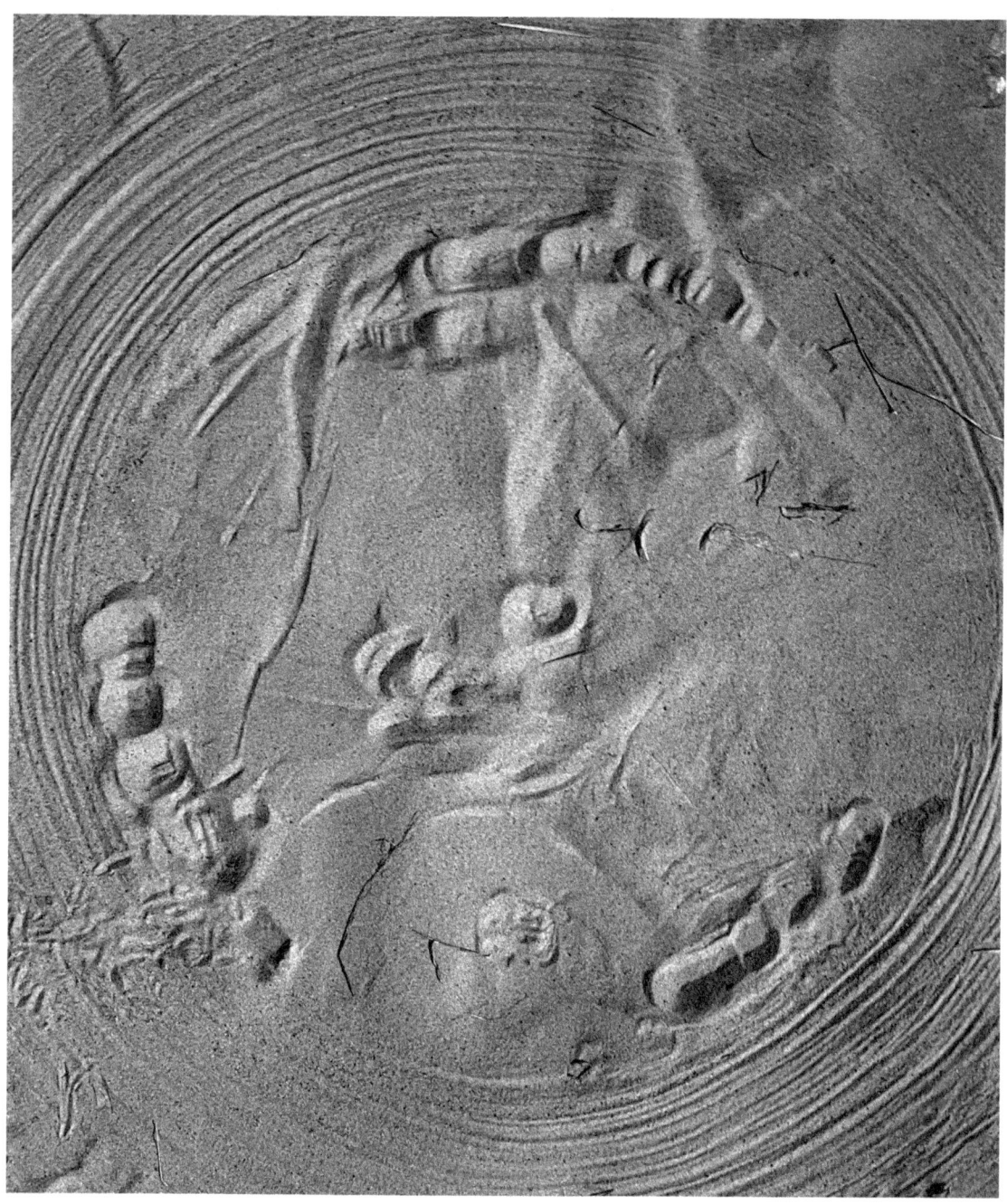

The project combines local material culture, participatory craft, and spatial sequencing to develop an adaptive coastal typology. Materials are sourced locally, with timber and thatch forming the primary palette. Reed grass cultivated beside the sea wall, is harvested by the community and processed into thatch for roofs. This cycle makes the wall both an ecological infrastructure and communal resource. Residents engage in maintaining and adapting the bothies, sheds, and the main hall structures, building resilience through care and repair. The architecture's take on the vernacular creates a familiar extension to the village in the face of an evolving landscape. Walkways tie the gradients of the programme together, passing through reed beds and across the wall, mediating between wet, dry, defence and dwelling. Together these methods create a living, participatory infrastructure where defence, ecology, and community overlap.

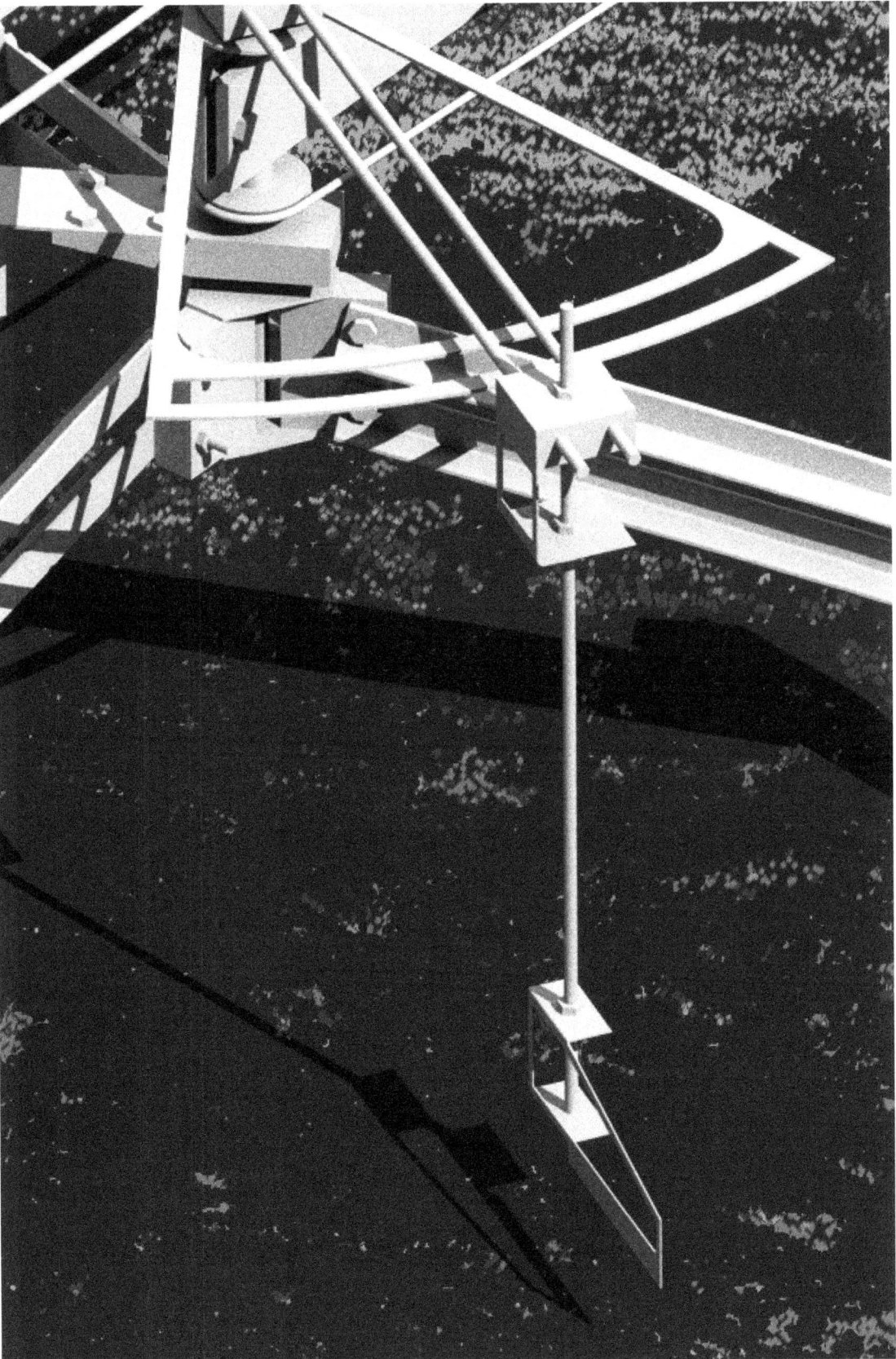

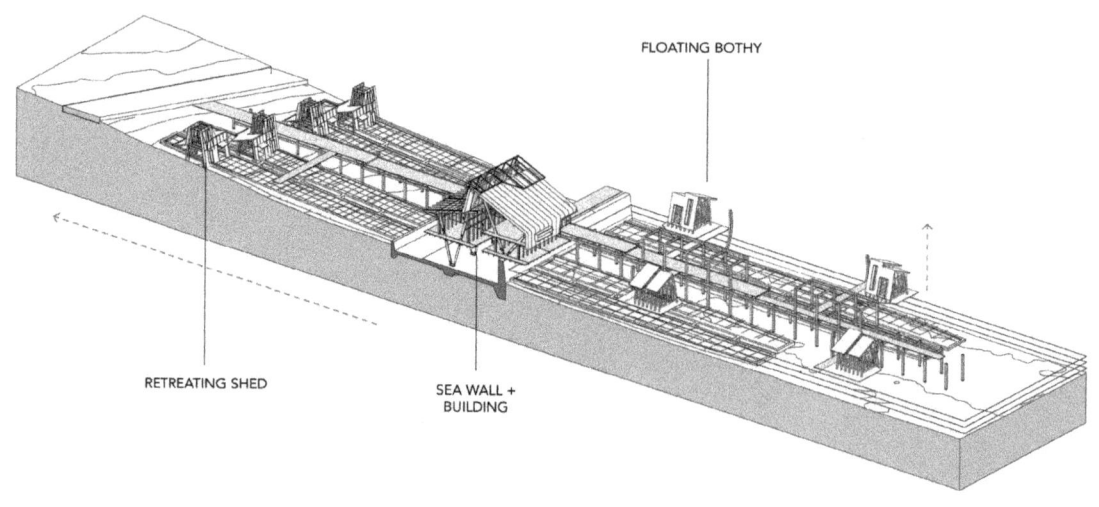

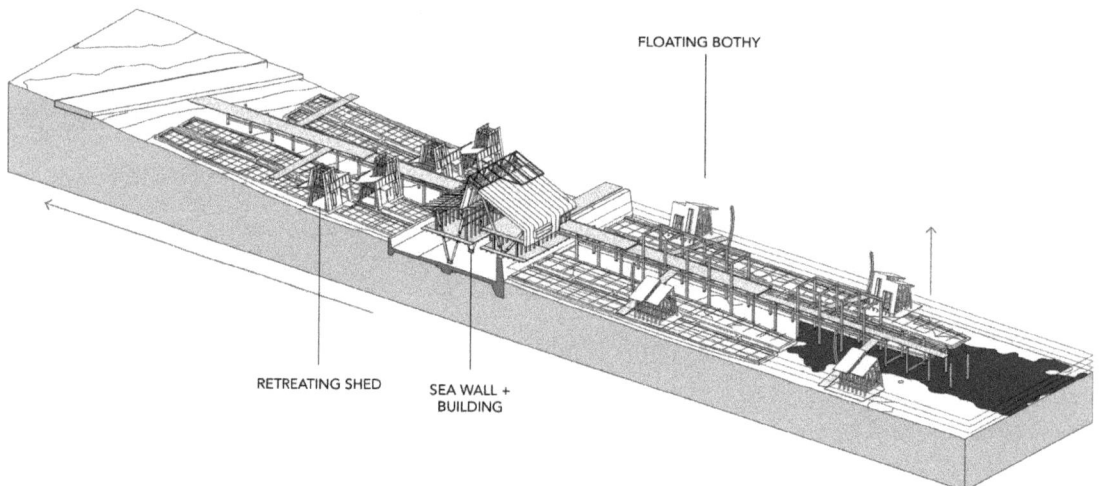

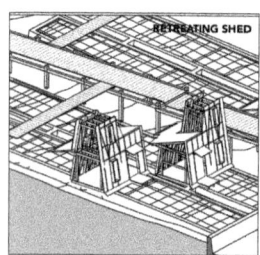 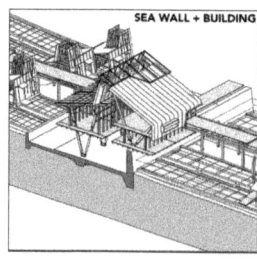 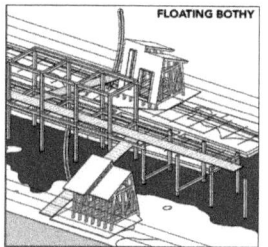

Project Images
Adaptive architectural interventions in reaction to shifting tides and future flood risk.

047 - 051: Sand Scraper performative device.
052 - 053: Architectural drawings tracing adaptations in response to shifting tides.
054 - 057: Physical model and visualisation depicting the proposal within its context.

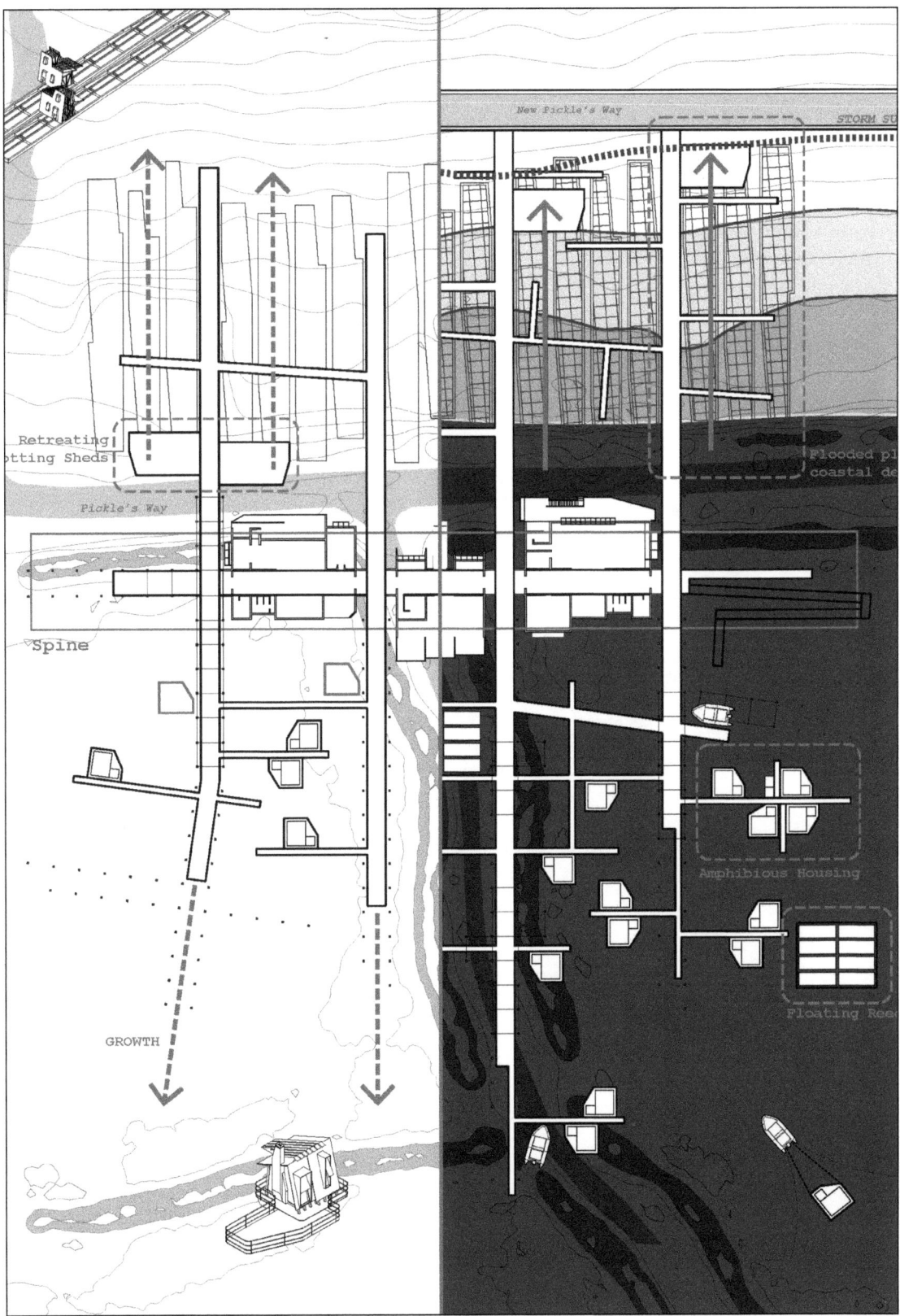

CLIFFE MARSHLANDS

REECE MURRAY

Cliffe Village, located on the periphery of London, is historically a working town, with part of the Marsh to the north once used for munitions production. This project proposes a community centre sited between Cliffe Village and Cliffe Marsh, offering a new way of thinking about how villages can develop outside of London's urban framework. It acts as a critique of current proposals for new residential expansion in Cliffe, instead giving residents the means and opportunity to shape the kind of village they wish to see.

The project is influenced by the history of Cliffe and its vernacular identity. It aims to provide the community with both the space and education to engage in construction and making, tying the development of the new Cliffe to ideas of community, circularity, and craft. By doing so, it invites reflection on the sensitivity required when intervening in landscapes at the periphery of London.

This discussion is particularly urgent in light of ongoing housing proposals. Redrow has recently been granted permission to construct 184 homes off Town Road, Cliffe Woods. Earlier applications for the site were rejected over concerns for bird habitats and inadequate bus services, though subsequent appeals and amended plans eventually succeeded despite more than 500 objections. As one councillor noted, "there is pressure to deliver housing, but also a recognition that there are better approaches." With over 700,000 homes planned on greenfield land despite capacity for 1 million on brownfield sites, Cliffe highlights the need for more thoughtful, community-led development.

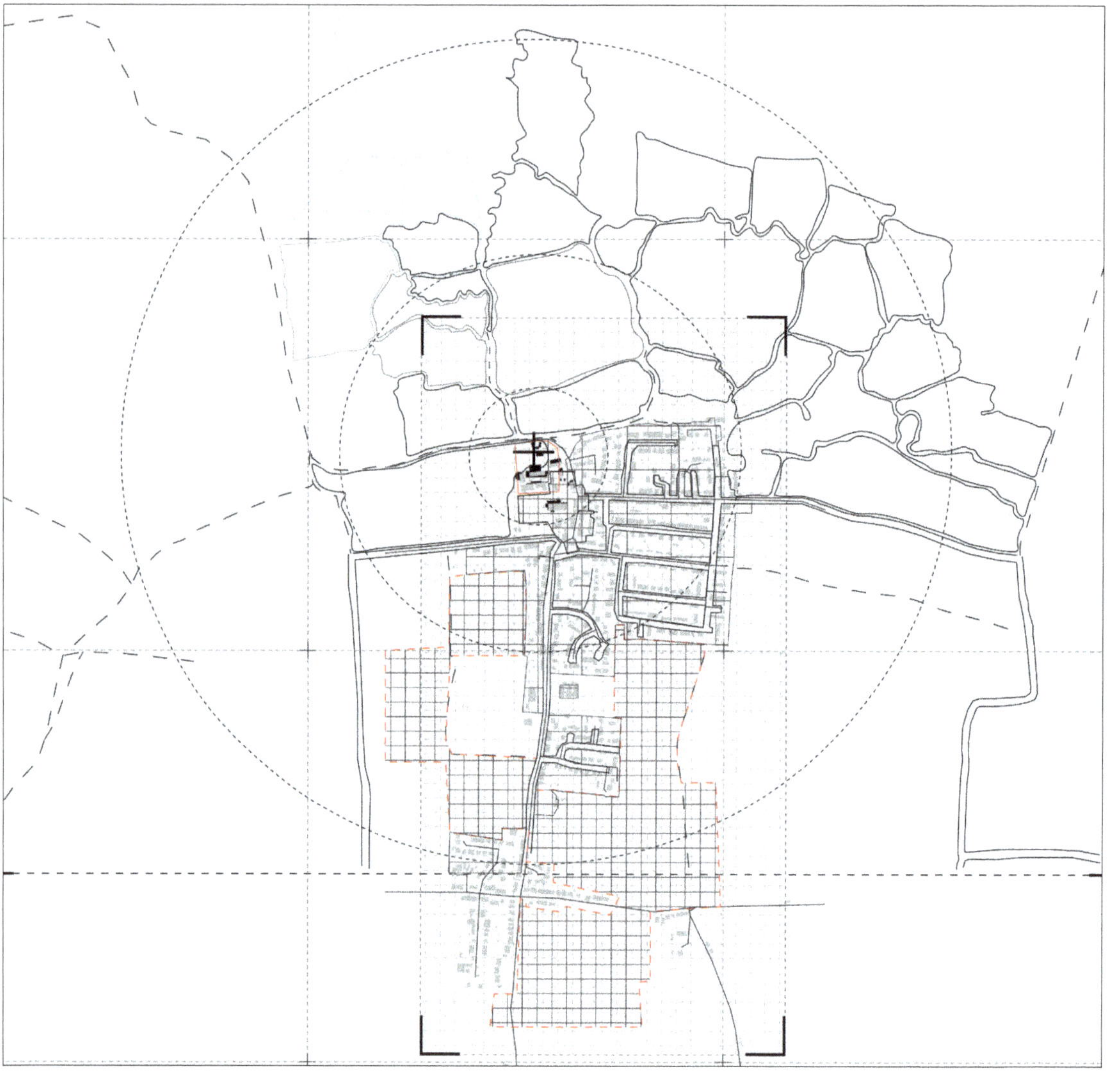

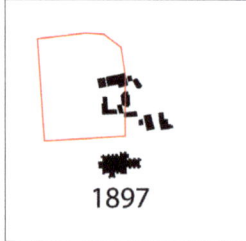
1897
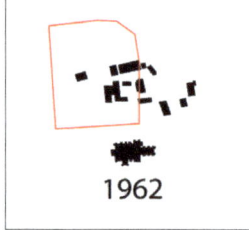
1962
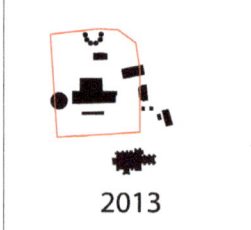
2013

Cliffe is defined by its extensive marshes, historically preserved for their potential use in port development. Much of the landscape consists of wet grassland, now managed as semi-natural grazing marsh for cattle, sheep, and horses. Today, tenant farmers maintain the land through Natural England's Higher Level Stewardship scheme, balancing agriculture with conservation. In the late nineteenth century, parts of the marsh were briefly occupied for munitions production. Though the industry was short-lived, traces remain in the form of derelict buildings, drainage channels, and spoil mounds scattered across the site. These remnants, while industrial in origin, now form part of the marsh's distinctive character. Combined with its ecological value, they support a diverse range of wildlife, contributing to the unique identity and layered history of Cliffe's landscape.

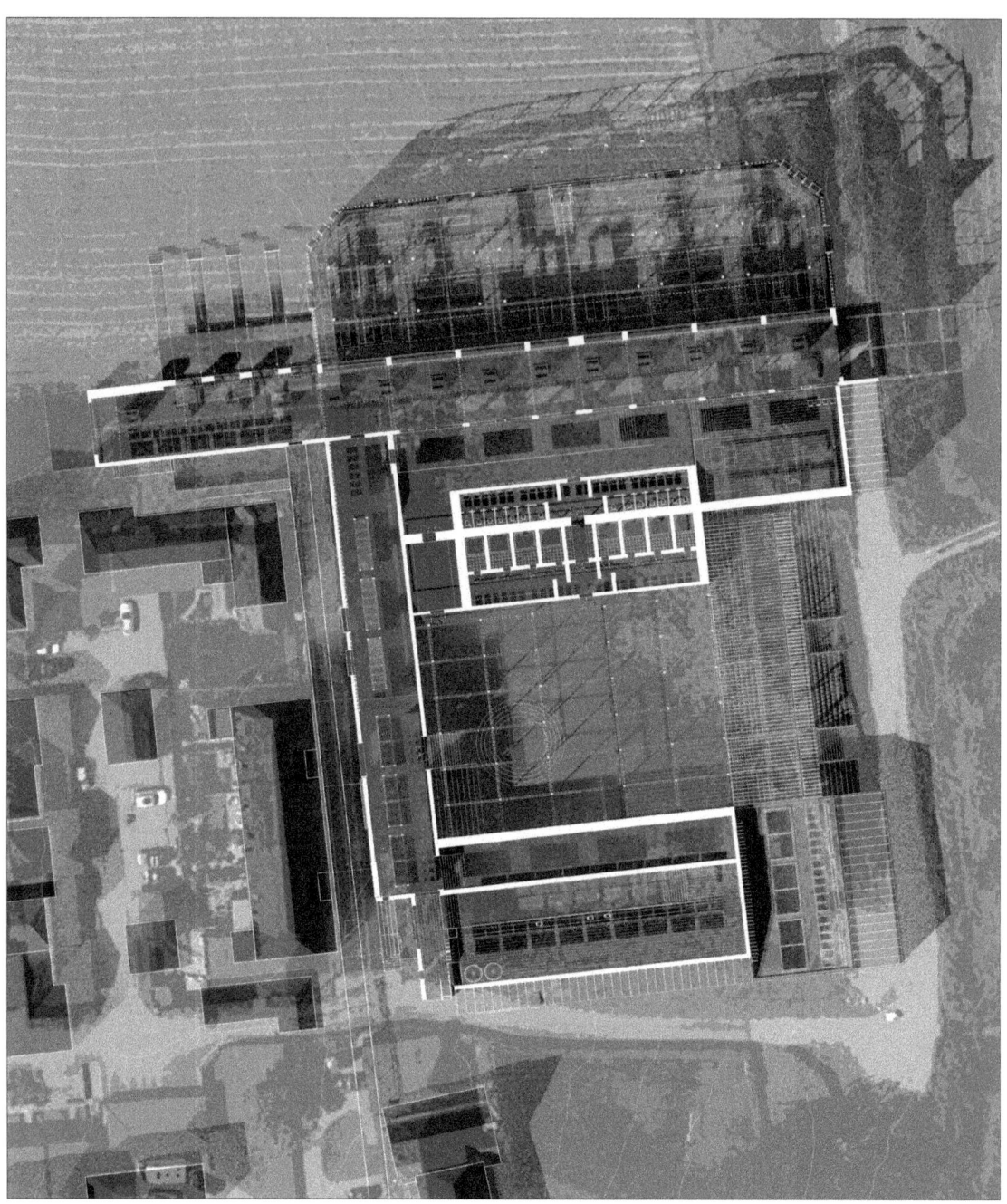

Commissioned by Medway Council, the project provides a community-led alternative to large-scale housing at Cliffe Woods. Community drives the design with residents participating in shaping the brief, governing the programme, and engaging in workshops and construction activities, ensuring the centre reflects local needs and skills. Circularity underpins the material strategy. Locally sourced components reduce embodied carbon, while construction elements are designed to be reusable, repairable, and renewable over their lifespan. The building responds to seasonal changes, allowing the fabric to adapt and perform year-round. Craft connects the architecture to place and tradition. Water reed from the marsh is used as thatch, Scots pine is sourced from nearby woodland, recycled steel comes from local industry, and rammed earth is formed from site excavations. This approach celebrates skill, materiality, and the tangible involvement of the community in shaping their environment.

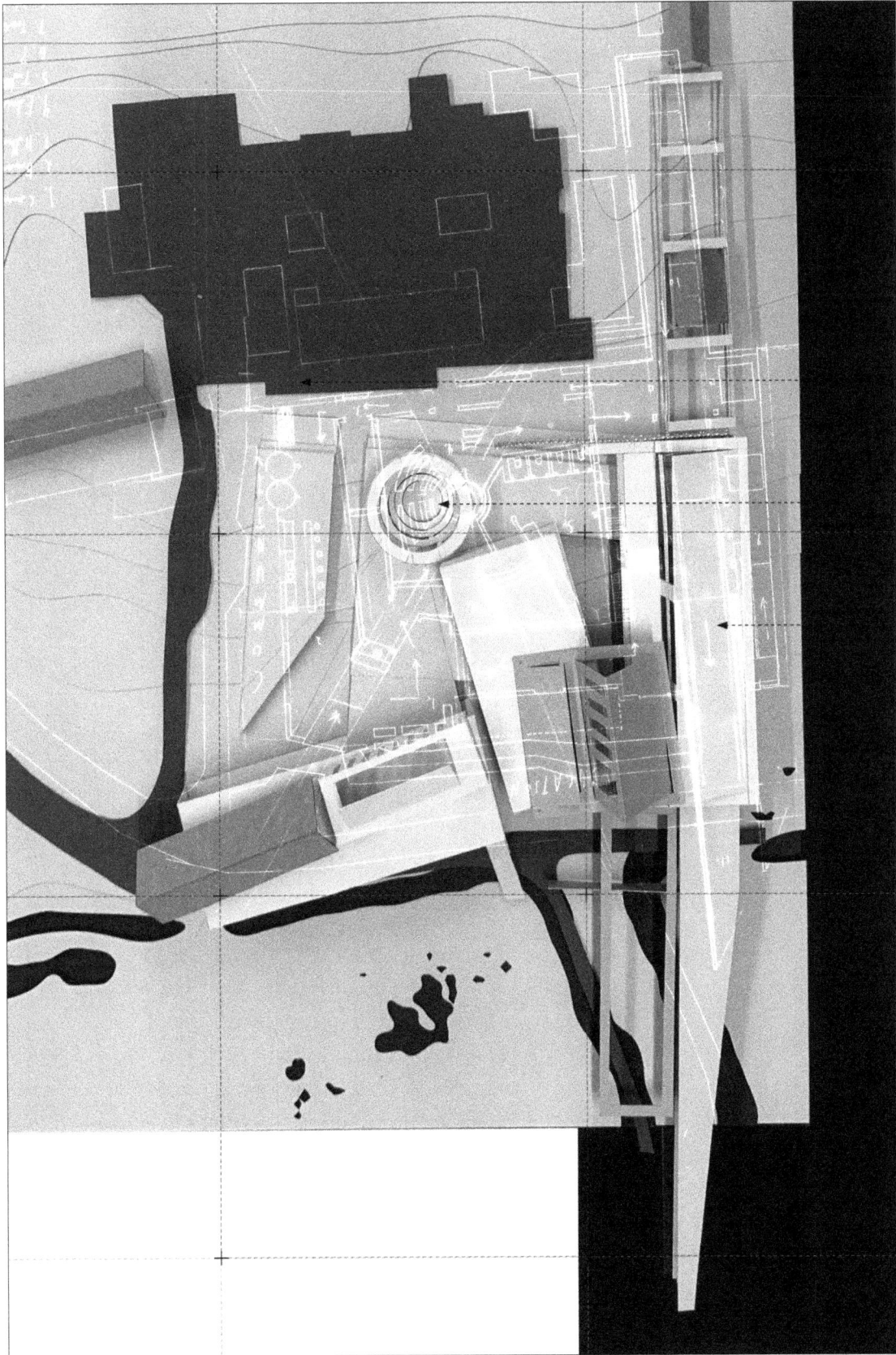

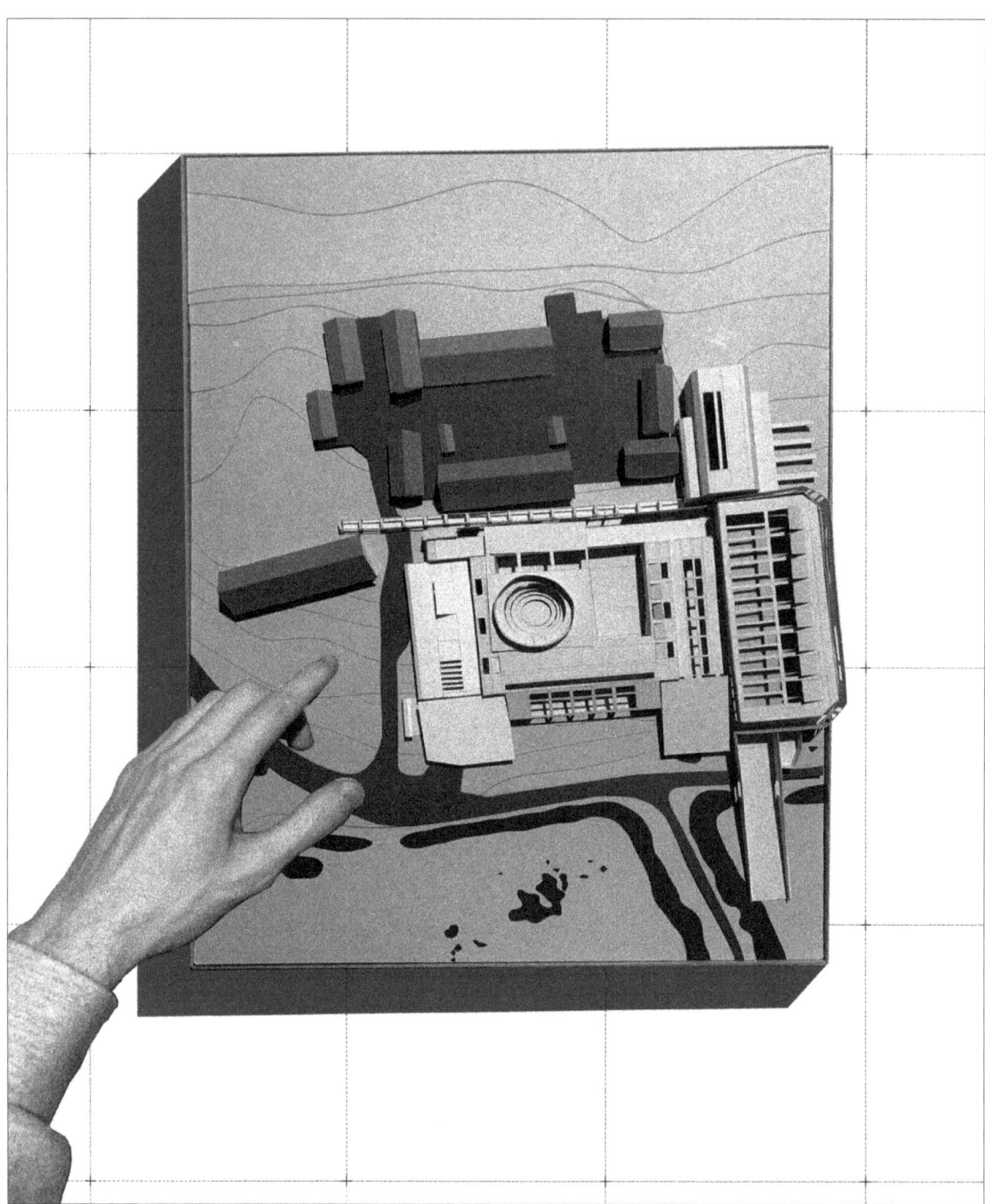

Project Images
Community-led construction and material centre testing alternative vernacular-led approaches to housing design.

059 - 061: The Clandestine, visualisations and spatial mappings.
062 - 065: Architectural development via drawing, model and digital compositions.
066 - 069: Detailed design and visualisation

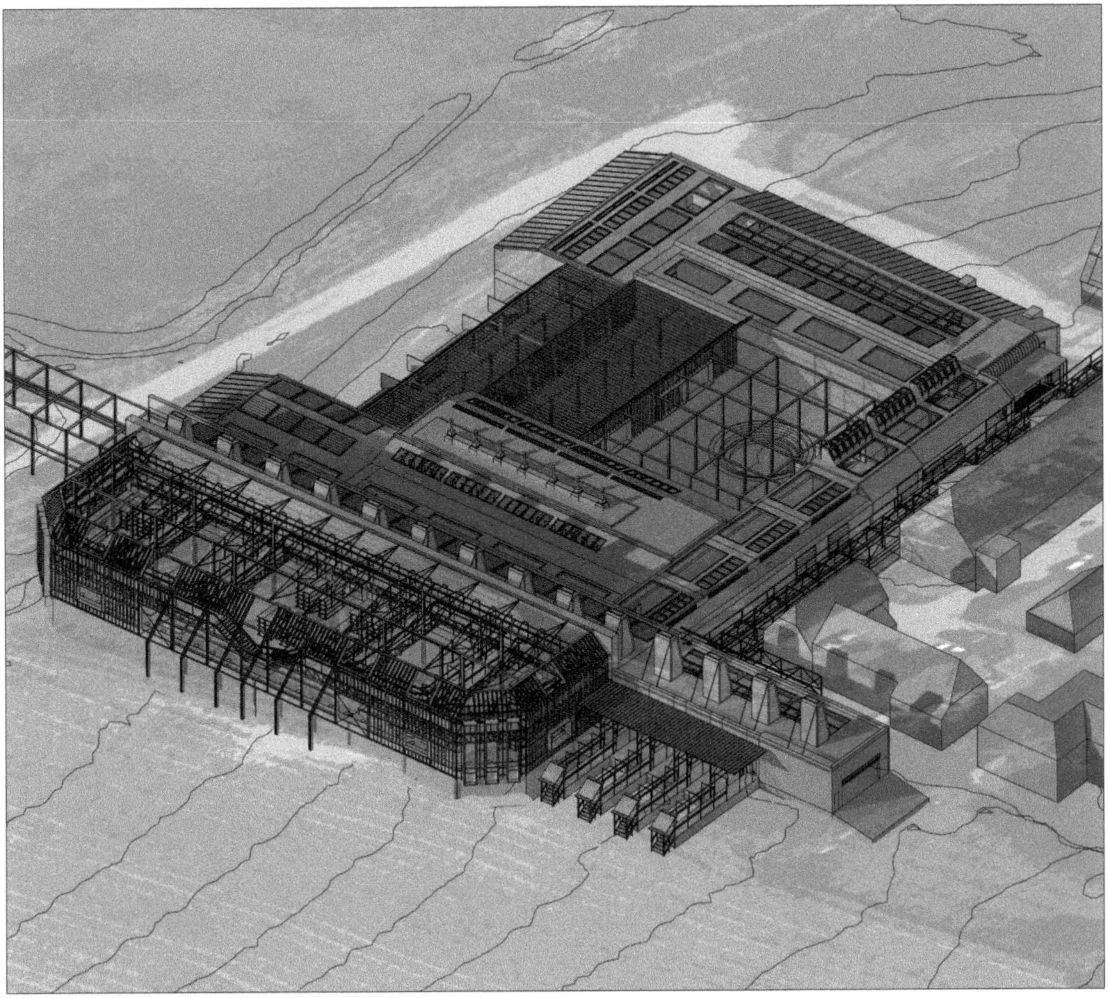

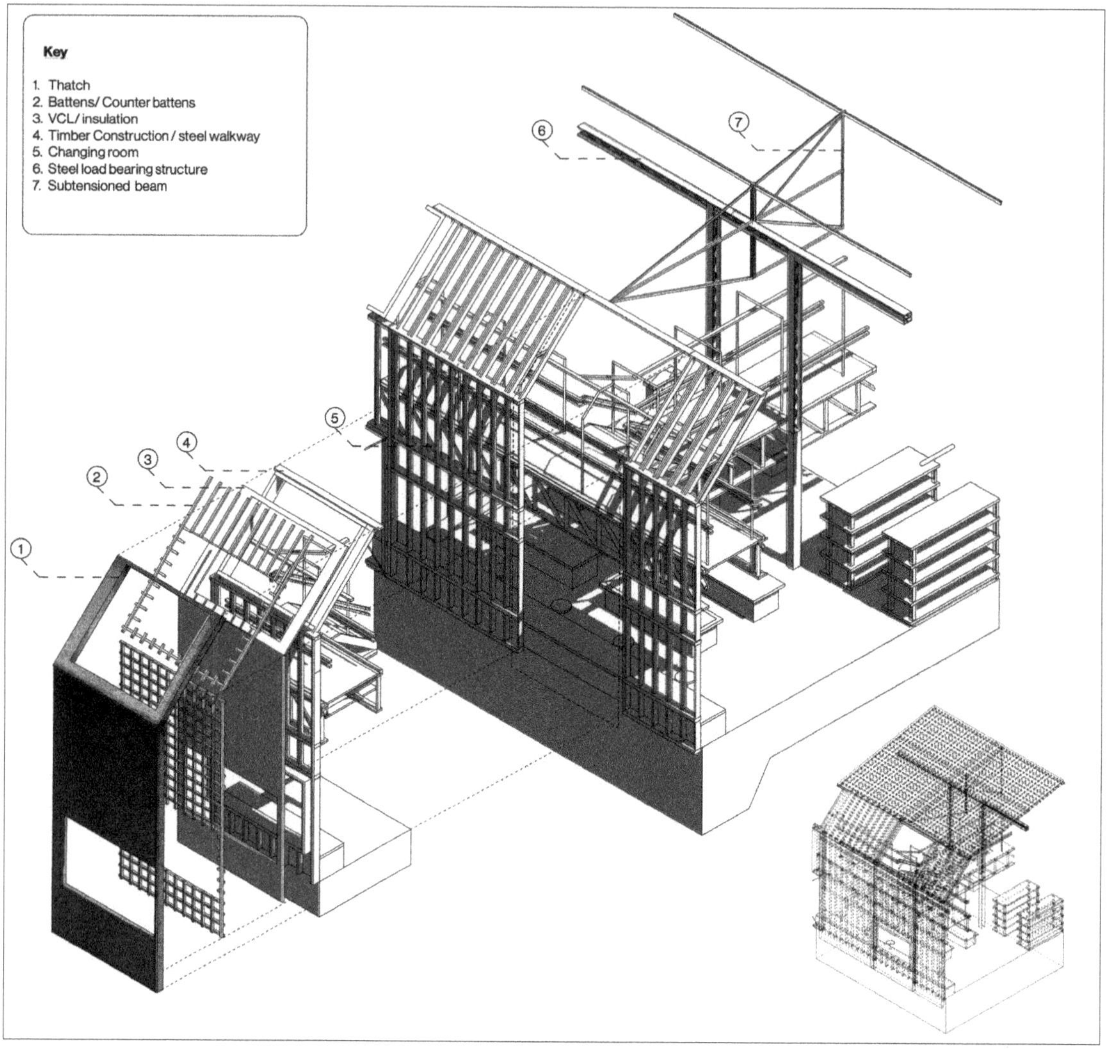

Key

1. Thatch
2. Battens/ Counter battens
3. VCL/ insulation
4. Timber Construction / steel walkway
5. Changing room
6. Steel load bearing structure
7. Subtensioned beam

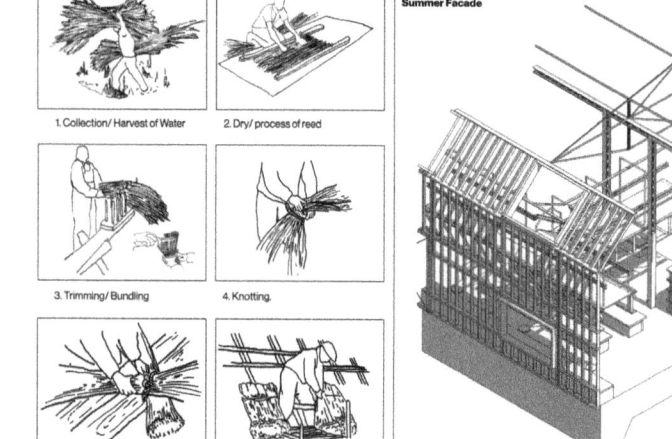

1. Collection/ Harvest of Water
2. Dry/ process of reed
3. Trimming/ Bundling
4. Knotting.
5. Application of thatch bundles.
6. Reed is laid like shingles

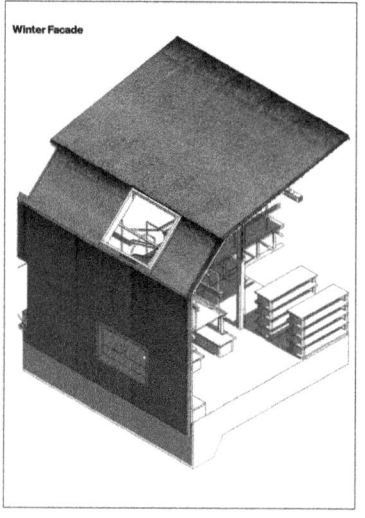

Summer Facade

Winter Facade

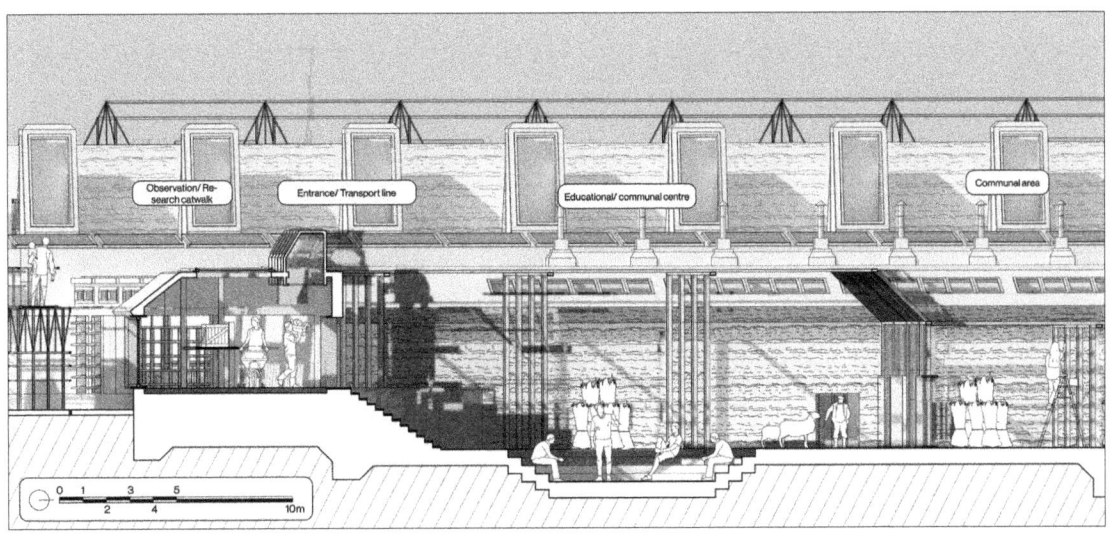

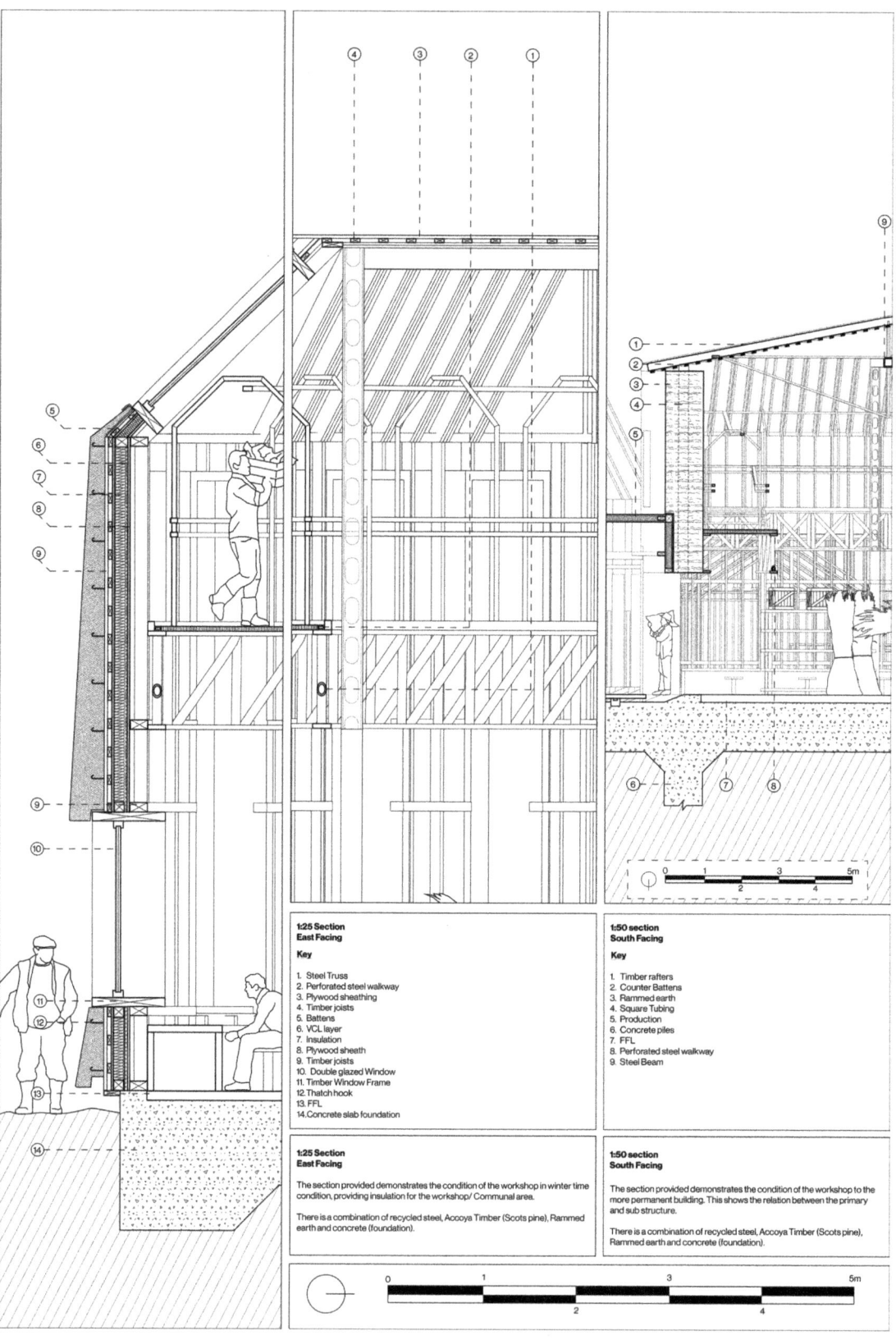

ON STAGING

PAOLO ZAIDE & TOM BUDD

The Hoo Peninsula offers a quiet but compelling landscape setting, where vast skies meet tidal mudflats and whispering marshes stretch out toward the estuary's edge. This is a place defined by stillness and subtle movement—by the slow rhythm of tides, the drift of sea-fog, and the flight of curlews over wind-bent grasses. Its flat, open terrain holds a sense of exposure and depth, revealing layers of time in the patterns of reed beds, the curves of creeks, and the shifting lines between land and water. It is a landscape shaped as much by memory as by geography, where every path or weathered fence seems to suggest a story held just beneath the surface.

Scattered through this quiet terrain are stage sets of human presence, man-made structures that stand like props in a long and complex performance of habitation, labour, and survival. Houseboats—some repurposed from old Thames sailing barges—line the inlets, offering a glimpse into a life afloat, past and present. Crumbling sea walls trace old battles against floodwaters, while derelict pillboxes and jetties mark the peninsula's wartime and industrial past. These structures do not impose themselves on the land; instead, they settle into it, part of a lived-in scenery where nature and history continuously overlap. Like the fragments of an unfinished play, they hint at the many lives and stories that have unfolded across this mutable edge of land and sea.

In landscape urbanism, staging emerges as a critical conceptual and operative strategy that reorients design away from fixed form toward open-ended process. Staging is not about delivering a resolved, static image, but about establishing conditions—a framework or milieu—within which temporal, ecological, and social forces can unfold in unpredictable, generative ways. It is the difference between dictating a final composition and orchestrating a dynamic field of possibility.

To stage a landscape is to choreograph its becoming, to recognize that space is performative and time-laden. The landscape is less a product than a platform for event and encounter, a medium through which ecological succession, cultural activity, and infrastructural transformation engage in continual dialogue. In this respect, staging is an embrace of contingency and complexity, inviting adaptation and inviting users to co-produce meaning and form.

This approach challenges traditional paradigms of planning and design, which often seek closure and certainty—fixed masterplans or formal solutions meant to impose order and finality. Instead, staging positions design as an open script, a provisional scaffold rather than a completed narrative. It gestures toward landscapes as processes, not objects; as evolving stories rather than conclusive statements.

ACROSS TIME: SEEDING, ACTIVATING GROUND

To engage in a process of staging across time the studio employs a variety of propositional methods. Through an activation of the ground plane to an understanding of the complex systems that shift and transform these landscapes, proposed form is seen as a malleable construct, informed from past notions and adapting to future predictions.

Seeding - Activating Ground
The use of quick, exploratory conceptual models act as a gateway into the design process. Beginning from the initial contextual ground plots and physical site catalogue, drawings and imagery are printed, cut and folded, creating a three-dimensional form from the flat ground surface. This intuitive process encourages experimentation and decision making through the act of construction. By working directly from the surface plots these models are able to activate these layers and explore proposed spatial forms through direct ground manipulations.

Settings
The work from the studio draws inspiration from a past wealth of culture and stories from the Thames Estuary, captured in the revolutionary paintings of John Constable and the celebrated scenes in Charles Dickens' 'Great Expectations'. This area has played as a backdrop for Kubrick's 'A Clockwork Orange' and 'Full Metal Jack', and conceals a stranger history of military training, gunpowder production, and chemical explosives works. This history and these stories give a strong setting to the projects and provide ingredients that inspire a unique approach and design language.

Storyboards
The studio seeks out novel and personalised methods of plotting of spatial narratives. These distinct settlements and landscapes are subject to endless shifting processes, both human and naturally driven which constantly transform these sites over time. The studio utilises storyboards and film as a medium to track and speculate on the future of these shifts. By approaching the proposition as an ongoing and experimental process, rather than a predetermined

one, we aim to learn from the natural, complex and unpredictable systems of the estuary.

The design methods explored through *staging* challenge the perception of the estuarine landscape as static. Instead, these sites are conceived as *"staging grounds"* that allow design to conceal, expose, connect, and unfold new possibilities. These approaches merge the technical constraints of a site with layered creative strategies. The *staged ground* anticipates gradual and extreme change, and the proposals here embrace flux, movement, and temporality. The writing, conversations, and projects suggest that the design proposals should not be viewed as fixed pictorial or typological solutions, but as frameworks—principles and guidelines—capable of seeding and activating the ground over time.

MALLEABLE LANDSCAPES

COLIN WALTERS

An interesting rhythm developed. Town quickly shifted to countryside, and after much pause, countryside yielded back to town. This cadence repeated between landmarks. In the pauses between, we were allowed space to think, to see, to hear. Objects in the estuary landscape were experienced more vividly, making the backdrop to our journey animated and lively.

For a brief moment, I was taken back to my childhood, where I would sit atop the hill in my backyard. From there, I would gaze over a rolling landscape dotted with barns and swaddled by forests. Between the clusters of trees were rippling fields, animated with livestock and peppered with bales of hay. These fields were canvases for my youthful imagination, the spirited backdrops for countless storylines. From the hilltop, I could dream.

Back in the estuary, our movement through the environment continued to activate normally stagnant characters. A pair of concrete bunkers shifted between golden grass and unruly foliage. Federal Sable, in her garish red coat, slipped down the Thames in the late afternoon sun. The old radar tower stood watch over the company, rooted to his position in the marshy flats. A chorus of windmills sang in the distance.

We were witness to the landscape's beautiful performance, simultaneously audience and director. As we meandered, objects within our surroundings were ever changing. Similarly, this essay will meander through varying viewpoints and perspectives, often shifting rapidly just as the landscape's actors appeared and disappeared from our sight.

Though the objects in the countryside leapt into performance, the actors at the beginning of our journey resisted us. Our call to movement was met by static streets. Each house imitated the previous. Beige, rendered exteriors faced their doppelganger across the road as far as the eye could see. Suddenly, at its edge, the town opened to empty fieldscapes. Uninspiring expanses surrounded the sleepy streets.

A STAGNANT SETTING

Bata Town is a foreign object in the wider estuary context. The railway is the sole lifeline of the townscape, the means of Bata Town's birth and its connection to surrounding villages and central London in the far distance. From the initial company town, a larger collection of houses, shops, and warehouses grew, becoming a layered urban fabric with many eras of construction. Yet, none of these eras looked further out into the landscape. Each drew a sharp line between town and country.

Like all of Tomáš Bata's company towns, this introspective nature is intentional. His modernist communities implemented efficient layouts, clean lines, and clear geometries, all subordinate to the shoe factory. In addition to industrial productivity, Bata cared deeply about worker welfare. Employee loyalty and well-being were foundational to company success. Housing, education, healthcare, work, and leisure could all be found within the town boundaries. By design, residents would depend on the town, devoting their lives to family, community, and the Bata brand.

Tilbury's Bata shoe factory closed in 2005, and so departed the very core of the community.[01] Today, Bata Town has lost its life, its purpose. It has gone to sleep. The artificial townscape sits against an unnatural patchwork of fields. Too stark a contrast exists between the built environment and the encompassing "natural" environment.

Indeed, even the countryside has its own distinct boundaries. Our preliminary walk revealed a large-scale figure ground outside of the town, an artificial patchwork of sharply bound fields that can barely be considered countryside. The fields have no relation except their adjacency, nor does the town interface with this land. Rather, Bata looks inward, sheltered from the dreary view by repetitive buildings, halfhearted fences, and disorderly treelines.

What Bata needs is a way to generate the missing scenery in the landscape surrounding the sleepy town. The fields are stagnant, their terrain and intrigue are flat. How can the surroundings become inspiring, vivid, or enlivening? What would it take to wake a sleeping Bata?

REPRESENTING LANDSCAPE

What creates the awe, the nostalgia, the wonderment, the curiosity, in any given artwork? Is it the objects, the scale, the color, the composition? Is it the soul of the artist, their message to the viewer, the context of the work? John Constable painted a well-established England, rendering rolling pastures with relation to an established settlement. Cows establish foreground before distant church steeples, farmers work a stone's throw away from their village, and billowing clouds envelop the viewer. Linear perspective dictates object scale, referencing a vanishing point off in the infinite distance. We see his scenes as we would with our own eyes, only they are depicted through lively brushstrokes.

Downriver from Bata Town, Constable captured the decaying Hadleigh Castle. Billowing clouds, blustering winds, and rippling grasses swallow the crumbling ruin. These forces of nature take on a celestial presence, as if the stony citadel is taking its last stand against the cosmos. The spirit of Hadleigh is echoed in the concrete bunkers we passed on our meandering estuary journey: man-made defense structures yielding to time and elemental strength.

Hadleigh Castle, John Constable, 1829 (02)

In the same time period that Constable worked, Japanese ukiyo-e artists were depicting their own landscapes through wood block printing. The scenes are rendered through layers of color rather than individual brushstrokes. Rather than linear perspective, artists like Hiroshige employed scalar exaggeration of certain elements in their compositions. Objects are not represented as the human eye would see it, rather, how we might feel the scene. There is an immediacy of all the elements in the image. Movement is demonstrated by animated figures, bending landscapes, soaring mountains, and swelling waves. The scale of the background is amplified; foreground and background are less distinct. Mount Fuji is a regular presence, often bigger than it would appear to the human eye. The landscape is an immersive tapestry, its edges somewhere out of frame.

I am reminded of *satoyama*, a Japanese term describing the occupied border area between mountainous wilderness and arable flatland, particularly in rural landscapes. Beyond its geographical definition, *satoyama* encourages a harmonious relationship between humans and nature. The land provides for its people, and the people tend to the land. I appreciate these rural villages. Buildings are scattered and their layout is energetic. Like Hiroshige's prints, the mountains soar above the rice paddies and houses.

The Sea off Satta in Suruga Province, Utagawa Hiroshige, 1858 (03)

The hazy boundary between field, town, and mountain reflects a distinctly Eastern way of seeing, favoring nuance over division. In such landscapes, spatial relationships are not fixed but malleable, a perpetual conversation between ground and its inhabitants. This sensibility extends beyond physical terrain into visual and built form, like ukiyo-e prints and winding gardens. Architectural historian William Alex beautifully contrasts Eastern and Western perspective in the opening pages of *Japanese Architecture*:

"The quality of depth in the East is perceived by a concentric rather than linear means, by patterns, vistas, or groups of vistas, horizontally or vertically extended or behind each other, rather than by direct means of linear perspective. In paintings as well as in gardens, there is a sense of immediacy and enclosure rather than a falling away in depth via outgoing converging lines or planes. Infinity is not a focused collection of distant points but exists somewhere outside of a series of concentric spheres, varying in atmosphere and content, their boundaries never very well defined, their range to be taken in at one's own speed, according to one's own inclination. Reality is to be apprehended by a process which does not extend logic but which deepens emotion." (04)

In the West, paintings are rendered as we view the landscape. Depictions of landscape from the late ukiyo-e movement instead ask us to *sense* the landscape. It's as James Corner suggests: a landscape is not just scenery, object, or thing but an environment within which the body is fully and completely immersed.(05)

STAGING A LANDSCAPE

Immersion into the wider landscape is exactly what Bata Town resists. One moves through its streets, but the body is not invited into dialogue with town or countryside. The setting remains fixed. Nothing shifts with perspective or reveals itself through movement. How can we identify and orchestrate the layers of town and country to bring life to Bata?

The earlier walk through the estuary made us feel as if we were both audience and director. Like a play, the journey unfolded with pacing and drama, shifting between tension and release, stillness and motion. Scenes revealed themselves with each step, as if the land itself were staging a quiet performance. If the ground is the stage, then the landscape becomes the backdrop, and architecture is the performer.

Great scenic design invites the body and mind into the world it constructs. A backdrop should immerse the audience and embrace the actors, actively creating atmosphere even when it recedes from attention. In *Asteroid City*, Wes Anderson crafts a desert town that is both hyperreal and cartoonish. The pastel buildings, two-dimensional rock formations, and endless horizon feel more theatrical than real, but they brim with story. Every element is exaggerated for mood, not realism. Like Hiroshige's prints, the scale and composition are felt rather than observed.

Live theatre embraces this same kind of spatial storytelling. In *The Lehman Trilogy*, a rotating glass box becomes home, general store, cotton field, and stock exchange. Each transformation unfolds in plain sight, as if the set itself is performing alongside the actors. In *Network*, flashing monitors, live-feed cameras, and massive video projections turn the stage into a frenzied television studio. The audience is not merely watching the spectacle, but find themselves caught inside it. These sets do more than depict location; they sculpt atmosphere and animate performance. They are dynamic landscapes that shift, breathe, and respond to the narratives they contain.

Not unlike screen and stage, we can begin to reimagine the spatial and emotional possibilities of Bata Town by becoming directors of the landscape's performance and artists of the ground's canvas. In addition to seeing what is there, we must sense what dormant relationships might emerge through the addition of built structure. To mature this directorial instinct, we can analyze existing scenes for their content and composition. The following four images are rehearsals: glimpses into how architecture, land, and historical perspectives might be brought into dialogue.

Bailey Preparation Plant over Enon Cemetery, Pennsylvania

Growing up, my imaginative innocence on the hilltop blinded me to fossil fuel industries around my home

These extractors gradually carved hundreds of miles of infrastructure on and below the earth's surface, drilling for natural gas and tunneling for coal. The epicenter of this activity is the Bailey Preparation Plant, a central processing hub that collects, cleans, stores, and ships coal extracted from three different mines. A cluster of coal storage silos loom over the Enon Cemetery, which is only accessible through the processing plant's entrance. The scale of individual and industry are in tension. A place of memory is dominated by machinery of production. In the center of the image, a conveyor belt pierces the tree line, forming a border between the silos and the cemetery. The belt shepherds coal from the northernmost mine, snaking nearly ten miles through hill and valley to arrive at the central hub. While souls rest in the foreground, nearly a hundred million tons of coal move through the belts and silos every year.

A Constable landscape extends beyond Bata Town's boundary

A contemporary street scene from the edge of Bata Town is interrupted by a superimposed section of John Constable's *Dedham Vale with the River Stour*. The insertion of the pastoral landscape—with grazing cattle, lush vegetation, and church steeple— feels like a theatrical backdrop lowered into place. A red British Railways logo floats absurdly in the field, marking a jarring seam between reality and performance. This collage proposes a speculative collision between the town's modernist present and an imagined rural past. The familiar grammar of Constable's idealized countryside interrupts the asphalt and pavement of Bata. It invites the viewer to think of the built environment not as a fixed reality, but as something re-stageable: nostalgic, performative, and dreamlike. The film-set quality implies the town could be re-scripted, as easily transformed as a theatrical production.

A narrow Tokyo alley unfolds in layers: utility wires and hanging clothes above, a delivery truck below, and dense facades compressing the view into a vertical, intimate corridor. Nothing monumental happens here, and yet the scene feels atmospheric. Like a Hiroshige print, the image draws power from composition and compression. Each object is casually placed, yet contributes to a choreographed whole.

This is an urban thumbnail of *satoyama*: not wilderness, but a gradient of the built and the living. The alley creates pause rather than spectacle. Its scale and texture invite the eye to wander slowly, discovering life in varied mundane details. The space is not decorated but inhabited, like a theatre set that comes alive when the actor—here, the viewer—enters and begins to move. If the Tokyo alley invites us to observe, this architectural model urges us to intervene. Here, the landscape is

An actuating model imposes 'satoyama' on Bata Town

no longer a static backdrop. It is pliable, staged, and speculative. The once flat fields of Bata are compressed into rugged terrain. Bata's rigid modernist houses are no longer inert objects; they are submerged into the rising mountains. This is *satoyama* not as pastoral nostalgia, but as deliberate regeneration: the countryside presses against the town, and the town folds back into the land. Like a film set, the scale is skewed and relationships are exaggerated. We are shaping atmosphere, conjuring dreamscapes around the sleeping Bata Town. In this imagined terrain, design becomes a kind of storytelling—one that reshapes memory, mood, and material. What other versions of Bata might emerge if we allow the ground to shift beneath it? If we are to reawaken the town, perhaps we must first reimagine the stage.

Urban 'satoyama' in a Tokyo back alley

WE CHOOSE THE LENS THROUGH WHICH TO VIEW THE GROUND

Bata Town faithfully realizes the ideals of the modernist perspective. Le Corbusier argued that a city should be a functional diagram dictated by logic and geometry.[06] Bata Town fulfills that vision. Though its layout is legible and efficient, the town lacks emotional or spatial resonance. It isn't an active scene. The viewer must work to animate the buildings, to coax them into performance. Rigid and resolute, the buildings stand against a landscape that is equally still. To connect town and country, we must complement modernist rationality with other ways of seeing—those that embrace atmosphere, memory, and the fluid dialogue between people and place.

Where Bata Town's logic imposes clear boundaries, other traditions and art forms invite a more immersive, relational experience. Constable's landscapes folded pastoral towns into sweeping hillscapes, capturing an intimate interplay of land and settlement. Hiroshige framed infinite space to pull the viewer through it, always moving. In satoyama, the built and unbuilt merge—a choreography between people, structures, and earth. The landscape, whether material or representational, is never merely a backdrop and actively influences its built forms.

A great backdrop creates a world for its actors, where they feel naturally at home. The relationship between land and architecture should be the same: forms feeling as if they have always belonged on the site, while the surroundings set the stage for their presence. As designers, our role is to listen and observe before engaging with an environment. By seeing the ground as more than just a site, architecture can harmonize with an animated landscape.

Notes

(01) Tim Burrows, *The town that Bata built: a modernist marvel on the marshes of Essex*, The Guardian, September 8, 2016.

(02) John Constable, *Hadleigh Castle, The Mouth of the Thames—Morning after a Stormy Night,* 1829, oil on canvas, Yale Center for British Art, Paul Mellon Collection; digital image, Wikimedia Commons

(03) Hiroshige, *Suruga Satta no kaijō / Hiroshige-ga (Sea at Satta in Suruga Province)*, woodcut print, *1858,* Fine Prints: Japanese, Pre-1915, Prints & Photographs Division, Library of Congress

(04) William Alex, *Japanese Architecture* (New York: George Braziller, 1963), 13.

(05) James Corner, "The Agency of Mapping: Speculation, Critique and Invention," in *Mappings*, ed. Denis Cosgrove (London: Reaktion Books, 1999), 231.

(06) Le Corbusier, *The Radiant City: Elements of a Doctrine of Urbanism to Be Used as the Basis of Our Machine-Age Civilization,* trans. Pamela Knight, Eleanor Levieux, and Derek Coltman (New York: Orion Press, 1967), 163.

Left:
Western and Eastern Perspective Studies based on the work of John Constable (top) and Katsushika Hokusai (bottom)

Left: Tilbury East edge condition
Right: Figure ground studies of Bata Town and of a Japanese *satoyama* condition

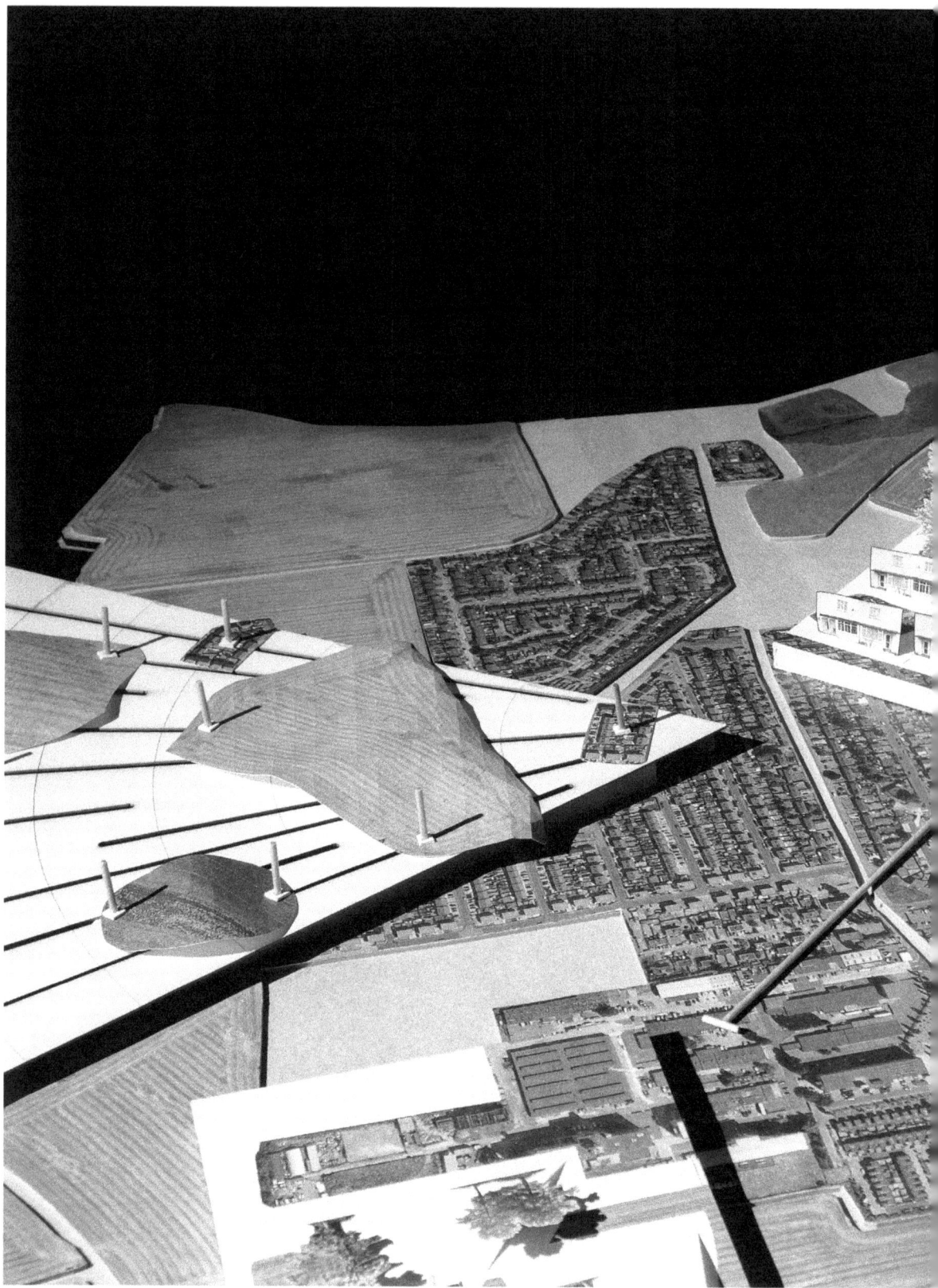

CONVERSATIONS

TOM BUDD WITH FORMER STUDIO 4 STUDENTS

ADELINA IVAN, AXELLE SIBIERSKI, IOANA ZAVOIANU, MARTA CONTENTE & PABLO PIMENTEL

WALKING THE EDGE

Tom Budd:
As a Studio we like to begin our initial investigations by framing the context of the brief. This is conducted through a site walk. When you began your project, how important was this initial walk, and the resulting mapping exercises within your work?

Marta
I think the walk and mapping of the site was a crucial start to everyone's project in our studio, although everyone interpreted it in different ways. This helped me connect the history and the sensory experiences of the site: the feeling of the wind, the earth, and the surrounding visual landscape. The observations of the stillness and chaos of the site, seen through the landscape and historic defensive bunkers became the start of the design process, using models and prototypes to capture and explore light, sound and texture.

Axelle
I began by looking at the relationship of the site between the water and the land, and understanding the human response to this built environment. This played a big role in how I continued the project, as it focused on this relationship in not just in the present but also the past. This led my research to an interview which, in turn, began to lead the project. For me, having that historical aspect to the work was really important because it began a process of storytelling. Being able to tell the stories whilst relating that back to the built environment and the relationship between water and land.

Tom Budd:
Did you find that some of these stories surprised you and how did these help develop your design practice?

Axelle
Yes, it definitely was something that surprised me. It was quite early on in the research process, I found an audio interview and wanted to be able to translate it visually and make it part of the project. That task of translation triggered a more intuitive response. Using my intuition and working by doing, as opposed to thinking led to a more organic process allowing myself to design without thinking too logically about the outcome.

Ioana
I think the walk was immensely important as it became the base of my first semester film, and resulting design project. The walk prompted me to compare the site to the psychological states of the people, which led me to look into literature, and authors writing about the landscape and the human condition. This inspired my animation work, which was essentially a reinterpretation of the initial journey that we took seen through a lens of the different qualities taken from literature.

Adelina
The site walk definitely influenced my work going forward, I think it set the base of my project. It allowed me to see the broader context of the area starting from Canvey Island, and through the walk to Southend. The first contact that I had with the site was Thorney Bay Beach with the blue wall, potted palm trees, and the plastic benches. I think this was already setting an idea in my mind of a very sterile, rigid and artificial environment, which developed into a theme that my project was critiquing.

Tom Budd:
How did you collect and record your findings on these initial walks and did these help to inspire new ways of understanding your design project?

Adelina
The studio proposed different ways of us relating to the site and understanding it, which I've never done before. I would usually take pictures of my project sites, but never tried to capture specific objects from the site. A few of us in the studio did this and made an object catalogue which allowed us to understand the site through a series of layers. In my work this directed the focus towards the thresholds between natural and artificial environments.

Tom Budd:
All of your projects were very much rooted in their context, learning from the history, tactile properties of the site and more fleeting moments captured through photography or film. Despite the common starting point it is interesting to reflect on how you all reinterpreted these initial findings and took them in unique directions within your individual design projects.

MODELS AND TRANSLATIONS

Tom Budd:
The studio works a lot through model making and this was often the medium that would translate your research and observations into more tactile propositions. How did you utilise the role of model making in your work, and how did this augment your design process?

Axelle
I think model-making played a really big part in my work and in me trying to trust myself to be more intuitive with how I designed. The use of paper as a model-making material, which I hadn't really used in previous years was helpful in this process. I think the speed modelling workshops we had at the start of the year really helped me loosen up my ways of working. Paper is so easy to use as a model making material and it's so quick that it meant I could develop ideas more fluidly from model to model as my design aspirations developed.

The making process brought an interesting spin on how I was trying to decipher the stories from the site recreate these visually. It was quite a challenge, because it was always hard to try and recreate such emotional and heartbreaking stories through visual means whilst ensuring you give it justice. Model making for me was a really key part of that, and is something I really enjoyed doing.

Pablo
I think that what helps me the most in the design process is model making. I've found that most eureka moments happen in the middle of assembling models, and making those models always starts with collecting fragments from the site. In the case of my first semester project those physical fragments came from the gas tanks and the debris from the Thames. I then used these fragments directly for modelling, reinterpreting them as new architectural elements which I laser cut and 3D printed to create a new catalogue of elements.

Once you have this catalogue of elements, you can begin experimenting, arranging and layering to create something new. It also starts defining the project and creating a framework or library of design moves, gestures and forms that I can return to through the design process. Once this framework is in place it becomes easier to start introducing new ideas or programmes.

Tom Budd:
It seems that through the act of making you were able to synthesise multiple strands of research and observations. How did this process help you translate these verbal, abstract or emotive elements of the work into more spatial propositions?

Axelle
The process helped me relate the story to the site, because there was such a large passing of time between the historic flood and our visit. On the site of Canvey Island there is such a strong separation from the human environment to the water due to the concrete defence wall. Through model making I was bridging this relationship and trying to understand the history and the contemporary context simultaneously. The model making was really helpful in merging the physical context of the area with the emotional context of the historic stories and interviews I was researching.

Pablo
From my experience, my interests focused on the relationship between industry, inhabitation and nature at Canvey Island, and how these three aspects of the urban realm coexist and collide right in the middle of this place. In London you have architecture that has been there for hundreds of years, almost fixed by history. But when you head east along the Thames Estuary you encounter scenes of constant regeneration, with places like Bata Town and the abandoned Calor Gas natural gas tanks sitting side by side with new developments. When you are there it begs the question, how did this collision of history and land use come to be?

With these questions in mind, I decided to collect fragments from the site as I encountered them. Some of these were natural things washed down by the Thames, but others were small industrial debris and household rubbish. At the time, the process felt random, but when I organised and laid these fragments out I realised that they represented my initial thoughts on the collision of industry, nature and domestic life.

Modelling with these fragments proved very important for the development of my project. I began by arranging them intuitively, without a clear goal, and through these tests it helped me grasp the connection between these forces in a more spatial way. These early models helped inform my final design. Modelling with these elements wasn't just helpful to inform the physical aspects of the design, but also because they helped me understand the historic layers and urban fabric of Canvey Island itself.

Tom Budd:
Sometimes the process of modelling is less about the final piece and more focused on the capturing of recording of these objects and the spatial qualities they present. How did you use models to experiment with the more experiential and fleeting qualities observed on the Thames Estuary?

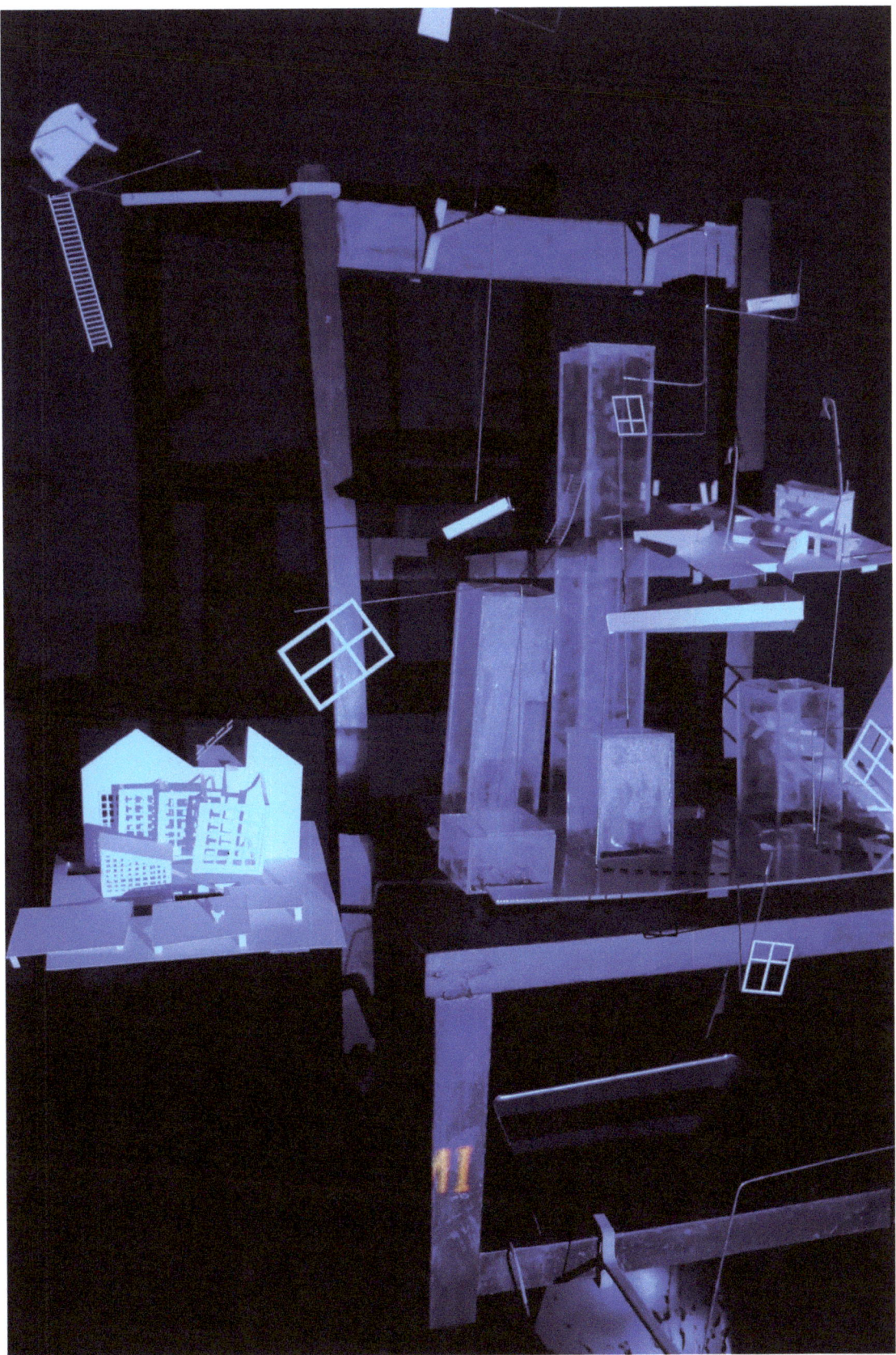

Adelina

It definitely helped me in the initial process, especially because I was initially very uncomfortable with physical model making, but ended up truly enjoying it in the end. The four or five observational models which I made during the first term were simply set up to translate what I observed on site. However, through the process of recording these I realised that they ended up behaving as small performances, inviting the observer to interact with these kinetic models.

Ioana

Model making was also not my favourite method initially, but funnily enough I see that some of my key design moments and best pieces of work came from those very early models. So I think the process of making these definitely helped me. They provided a very simple formwork, and with the addition of candlelight and sound became the first experiments with filmmaking, connecting these moments into my larger design project.

Tom Budd:
Thinking about the crafting of scenographies for your project, what role did the idea of stages or staging play in the development of your ideas?

Ioana

The idea of staging and stages was very dominant within my project. The work looked to produce atmospheric moments of scenes within the design, thinking of these as stills in a film. This led to the creation of a sequence of moments and spaces that evolved into my project.

NATURAL AND CULTURAL RESOURCES

Tom Budd:
We have spoken a lot about the process and ways you have all approached your projects. Opening this out to wider themes across the studio there was a strong focus on materiality in the work, through physical tests and technical investigations. As the natural and cultural resources along the Thames estuary are not inexhaustible, how did your project address questions of material ecology?

Adelina

Yes I think my project definitely touched upon material ecology. I think the material dimension of my project was addressed both through circularity and craft in the programme of the building. The project was focused on the relationship between nature and humans, and I focused on materials that would not deplete the environment such as timber, rammed earth and thatch. Thatch in particular feeds into this narrative of circularity as it's a renewable material and it also made sense with the site, as the new proposal was introducing these agricultural patches where crops could be cultivated. The thatch had multiple purposes within the building, using it for the roof and the wall insulation.

This idea of circularity came from the fact that the thatch and the building itself were not meant to be permanent. After around 20-30 years, the thatched roof needs to be removed and replaced. The intention was that the thatch would be grown on these agricultural land patches, then harvested and used to replace the old roof. This was mainly informed by the Ise Shrine in Japan, which is faithfully rebuilt every 20 years to pass on the tradition and craft from one generation to another.

Tom Budd:
There seems to be this shared theme of you designing through time within the studio. This was explored at a variety of different scales from the change of a site within a day, to a change in a landscape over 10, 20 or 30 years. How did these investigations of time scales and cycles affect your work?

Axelle

This was something that I really tried to bring forward in the work, because I thought the passage of time through a day was quite interesting. How does the experience differ, depending on the time of day you would witness it? I did a lot of research on potential rising sea levels in the North Sea due to ice melt. A key part of my drawings were adding those sea levels and understanding how these changed over the course of a day, and what you would experience as the user depending on when you were to visit the proposal. At low tide there would be passages revealed made of oystercrete and shells from the fishing industry. These would allow you to walk just above the water, like a pier where you could discover the water like you would discover the earth. At high tide these passages would disappear, and as the building was made of elevated timber volumes within a structural steel frame, you would suddenly be floating just above the water looking down on it.

Tom Budd:
When designing with time and circularity, the way we work with an existing environment and community becomes a key consideration. How did these factors influence your work and what are the key considerations you try to take into account when approaching a design project?

Marta

Yes, that's definitely something I've also encountered within my own work and in practice. It feels like it is becoming a point where ecology and environmental design have been turned into a trend. They want to make projects workable and green, but then there is a massive highway in the middle.

In my work I tried to focus on ways to help the environment and allow it to thrive. It seems that the way it's actually being dealt with in contemporary practice is to just meet specific guidelines or as an element that is just for show, and it's a bit sad. But again, it makes me hopeful that this next generation is going to turn that around and push for real change in this area. Creating projects that are actually trying to benefit the environment and working with the elements we have rather than just building, demolishing and building again.

Pablo

I think one of the biggest realisations, and disappointments, when I started working was coming to terms with the limitations of an architect's power in the real world. I certainly miss studying because I think when we're studying architecture at university, you really see the way in which we can have an impact, you're encouraged to imagine big, to believe in the potential for meaningful impact.

Coming from the Dominican Republic, I've seen first-hand how architecture can make a difference. Kids studying in shacks with dirt floors, and how even the simplest intervention can transform their lives, their outlook. You don't need massive resources to make meaningful change. That's what makes the architect's role so powerful, and why it matters deeply what, and for whom, we design. The cultural and social life of the user should always be at the heart of our work.

So, when I found myself working at a big commercial practice, it was a bit disheartening. You realise you're designing for the ultra-wealthy, people who often don't care about the environment or social impact. It felt like the opposite of democratic architecture. But that experience also gave me a kind of moral clarity. It made me more determined to go back, to re-engage, to fight for architecture that actually serves people who need it.

I've also come to realise that the process matters as much as the outcome. I believe in designing from the bottom up, starting with materials, sustainability, and the needs of the people who will use the building. Too often in practice, we start with a flashy form, a volume, a massing, something "cool", and only later try to retrofit the environmental or social layers. That's backwards. We should be asking from the start: What sustainable materials can we use? Who are we designing for? How can we make this building as democratic and accessible as possible? Once those questions are answered, then we can begin designing. Or at least meet somewhere in the middle.

SENSE OF PLACE

Tom Budd:
I think an amazing part of architectural education is the diversity of opportunities, places, people, and experiences you can learn from and help you develop your own unique approach towards design. This concept of a personal and individual design response is something we have tried to champion within the studio.

Reflecting back on your time in the studio and the work you produced, what are the learnings from your own design project that you have taken forward, and now that you have been in practice how have your ideas changed?

Adelina

I didn't necessarily find it different from what I imagined, because I had worked in architectural practice before. But I wasn't surprised, because I think the way I understood my project was more as a commentary or a critique rather than something fully grounded in reality.

Now I am studying for my master's degree, I'm definitely carrying forward some of the themes that I explored in my 3rd year, for instance, this very focus on nature. I'm currently looking at a project that explores the forest in Romania, trying to understand this through multiple layers. The forest as a resource, the forest as a crucial space for maintaining biodiversity, and finally the forest as a space for spiritual practices. The relationship that people have with timber is very important in my work. In my 3rd year I just considered this to be a renewable and almost disposable material, but now I'm understanding the bigger picture, and that just because it's renewable, it doesn't mean it's endless. You can't produce a forest simply by planting trees, that's essentially just a tree plantation. By moving away from this dimension of wood as material, and perceiving it on a different level now in my masters, it's exciting to still be exploring these similar themes.

Ioana

My design project made me realise what I want to do with my life. I would really like to have my own practise as an architect, but I also want to design experiences, making set designs, fashion shows, concerts and exhibitions.

Axelle

I think for me architectural practice is definitely quite different as I am working in commercial architecture. When I was at university, I was very keen to work on commercial

projects, as I thought that that's where the most creativity could happen. The budgets were bigger and this could lead to more freedom. However having worked on these projects you realise a lot of the nice design you do in the early stages can sometimes get taken out through value engineering. It's very easy to over design when you're in those environments, and I think it's definitely shifted my perspective on what I want to do.

Going forward, I value contributing to communities and designing for the people that ultimately will use the buildings. I definitely would now be more selective with the sort of practices I would like to work at. Having worked in a commercial firm I've realised why it doesn't really fit who I want to be as an architect. I think for the future, I would like to qualify as an architect, but I don't see myself working solely in practice. I have a keen interest in research and would like to develop this alongside design to contribute to the good of architecture in the future.

Marta

When we come straight from university we are very hopeful about what we would like practise to be. One main thing that I would like to bring more into practice is making and drawing with your hands rather than going straight into the computer. It just feels very inhuman to use a machine straight away.

I think there's a lot more to this than the bureaucracies, and it is important to be able to speak to the people that are going to be using the building and really understand what these people actually need rather than what will make the client money. If I could start my own practice I would like to humanise this process of design.

Tom Budd:
When developing a design project, we often draw from a variety of sources to help inform and inspire the work. In the studio, we encourage students to bring in their own personal experiences to help enrich the work. How did your own personal interests and background influence the direction of your design project?

Pablo

Looking back, especially at my Semester 2 project, I can now see how much it was shaped by the idea of democratic space, even if I didn't fully realise it while I was designing. The building was conceived as a shared environment, with very little private space. Everything, on both the urban and architectural scales, was communal.

At the urban level, I designed a large public park, a space open to everyone. And within the building itself, that idea of sharing continued: communal farming areas, shared living spaces, a swimming zone, an art gallery, a theatre. It wasn't just about the programme, it was about creating spaces that encouraged collective use and ownership.

That theme tied back to my first semester project, which was about company towns and the idea of shared resources within a built environment, but it was also personal. Growing up in the Dominican Republic, I was surrounded by architecture where the line between inside and outside is blurred. That sensibility found its way into the project, especially in how the building interacted with nature, opening up in the summer, closing in the winter.

So, on both a design level and a conceptual one, the project became about openness and accessibility, about creating architecture that's democratic, responsive, and shared by everyone.

Marta

Within my project the engagement of buildings with nature is something that I grew up around in Portugal. References in Portugal like the Leça de Palmeira pools by Álvaro Siza. I enjoy these big design moves that feel very unnatural, but then they somehow interlock and work well with the natural environment. These pools are made from harsh concrete shapes that create strong shadows and pockets of moments that feel explorative. This reminds me of my childhood and just spending time outdoors.

I think the field trip that we did to Rotterdam also helped a lot, especially the visit to the Waterline Museum which became a huge driving force in my project. These examples of big, bold design moves that cut through the earth are a really good embodiment of what I was trying to convey in my own design work.

REFLECTIONS

Tom Budd:
Reflecting back, can you summarise which moments from your time in Studio 4 had the biggest effect on you?

Adelina

The first would be the studio field trip to Vienna, which is where most of the bonding between the studio happened. Although I had been to Vienna before, it was such a valuable time for me also as I had never been given such a thorough architectural tour of the city. The sketching exercise we carried out using the little passport notebook from Muji, and sketching not only the spaces we visited, but also the architectural elements which we could not see in those spaces, such as a door's mechanism in section rather than a perspective view of a room. I think this helped me think of my surroundings differently and it stuck with me in the long run. Whenever I go on a trip now, I buy a little Muji notebook and I draw what speaks to me.

The second very impactful moment was the end of

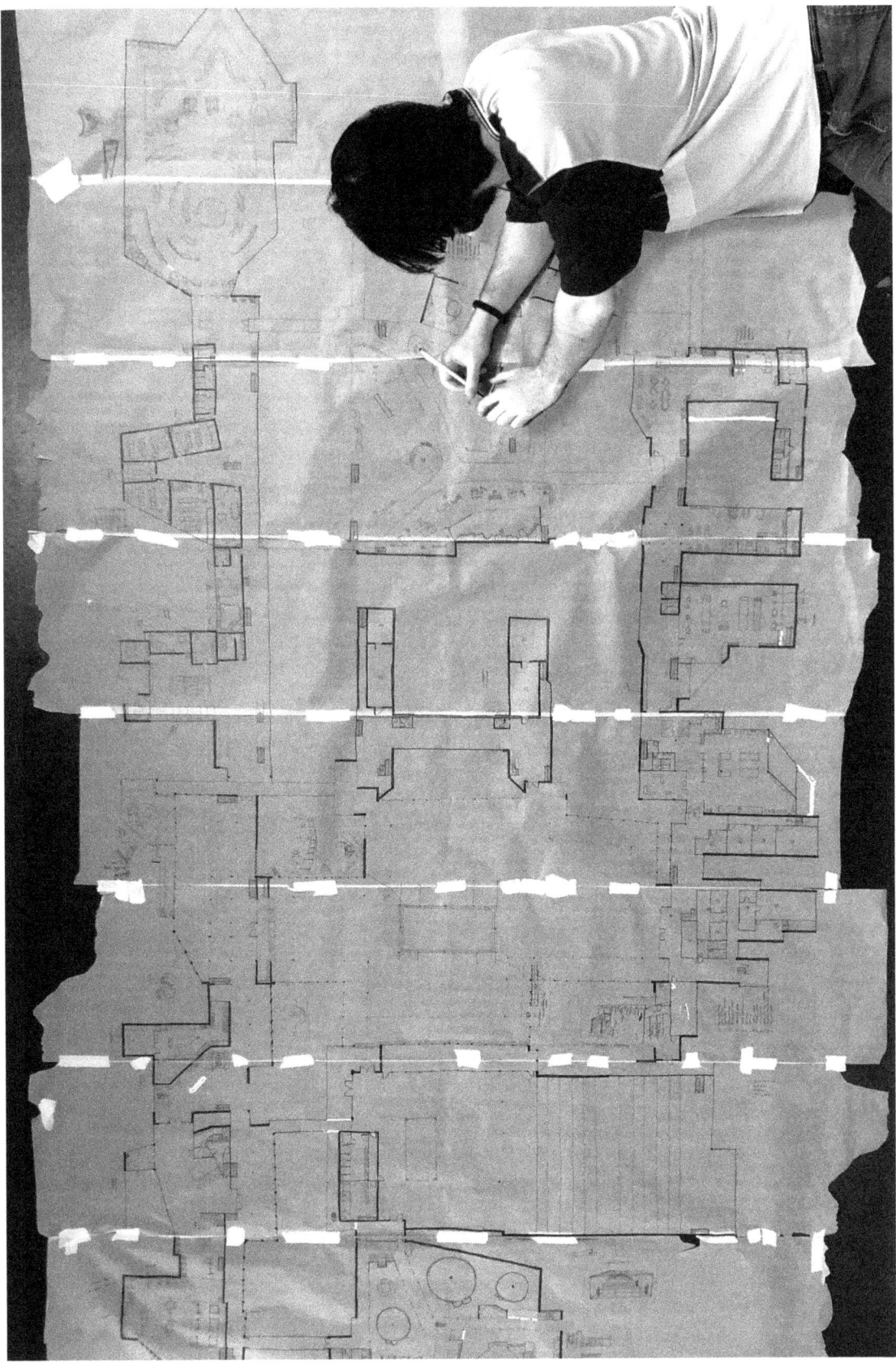

year exhibition. While those two weeks were more stressful than the whole year, I think it was an amazing experience to have. It was me and Nausheen who were curating the exhibition wall, and as someone that had never done that before, it felt like a very big responsibility. But I found it to be so incredibly useful and, as stressful as it was, I would repeat the experience a hundred times. It was also such a bonding moment between everyone. I remember a few hours before the opening, we were all preparing the booklets and the long sectional drawing, which ended up being so great.

I'm quite individualistic about my work and enjoy doing everything by myself, but for an exhibition one obviously can't do that. So I was put in a situation where I had to work with those around me, and it ended up being amazing. I think when so many creative people come together, the energy in that setting is so special and cannot be matched by anything else, and for that reason I dearly value those two weeks.

Ioana

I think I think the exhibition was a great introduction to life working in practise. Everything is about coordination and communication. You realise that you have to speak to that person to make sure everything gets done in time, there's so many similarities to how actual practise life is every day.

Marta

Yes, I think in our year a lot of us showed up consistently and were very invested in the exhibition. This was really nice because you see everyone putting forward their best work and see how everyone's different designs and methods came together come together into a unified show space. This worked particularly well in the poster Ioana and Ray helped create which managed to make the visual work flow from one to another despite the work having different narratives. There was something that definitely united us as a studio.

Axelle

I definitely echo what is being said about both the experience of the show build and the field trip, especially the trip to Vienna. I think that was a really key bonding moment for all of us, and actually made the studio what it was. It's one thing being in the studio with everyone when you sort of don't really know them, but I think it became a whole other experience when we had bonded as a studio, and we were all there together. The key moments were, for me the late nights, or even when we were there all day, and there were so many conversations had about other people's and our own projects and asking opinions, and I think for me, that was really valuable, having other people's insights,

and being able to ask questions to my peers.

Those two moments really stood out, and for me being in the studio was something I enjoyed, and actually something I really miss. I think having that space that is ours that we could be fully creative in, was something I found really valuable. This was a key part in creating that bond with my peers, and also my tutors.

Pablo

For me, what really defined my undergraduate experience was collaboration. I know it sounds a bit cheesy, but it's true. Those late nights in the studio, everyone there at 1:00 a.m., completely immersed in their work, there was such a unique energy. Someone would come by, look at your drawing, and say something like, "Why don't you flip it upside down?" You'd try it, and suddenly it just worked. That kind of spontaneous feedback was amazing.

It wasn't just about working alongside your own studio group. You'd wander into someone else's space, like Constance's studio, and ask, "Hey, what are you working on?". You'd see a model and think, that's amazing, maybe I can try something like that. It was this constant exchange of ideas, informal but super inspiring. There's nothing quite like being in the studio late at night surrounded by people with the same creative energy and determination as you.

Tom Budd:
I think that's a really nice place to finish up. I completely agree, the studio is such an important part of your learning, and I always say that you learn just as much if not more from your peers than from anywhere else. It is so important just to work in a space where you're surrounded by like-minded people all the time, and it makes the journey that much more exciting.

Thank you all for your insights and reflections and we look forward to seeing you develop into inspiring Architects in the future.

Conversations

Images of Design Process

87: Bodhi Horton Field Study Hoo Peninsula 2021
89: Axelle Sibierski, Memories within Water Installation 2022
91: Marta Fernandes Contente, Terra Citadel, Model 2024
93: Eric Turner, Post-Scarcity Sinecure, 35mm scans & cyanotype prints, 2023
95: Raoul Tomaselli, Suburbia Test, Plan Drawing 2023
97: Studio 4 - Group Show Film Still

COLLECTIVE HARVEST

ADELINA IVAN

"Collective Harvesting" addresses the slow erasure of Southend-on-Sea's raw coastal identity, following its recent elevation to city status in 2022. The project is an exercise of reimagining the city's car parks in the interest of the community as places for growing, learning and making.

The project themes integrate new areas of urban farming, communal cooking and dining, together with library and workshop spaces, therefore behaving as a new 'piazza' for the city. The community is encouraged to directly engage with all farming processes, from planting the seeds to ploughing the ground, harvesting the goods and storing them away from winter.

Apart from planting, growing and cooking crops on site, a defining element in terms of circularity for this project is that of the thatched roof. The thatch can be cultivated within the newly designated agricultural zones, subsequently harvested and then used not only for roofing, but also as insulation for the building's thermal envelope. The prioritisation of raw and minimally processed building materials further feeds into the proposal's narrative of superimposing natural elements upon the hyper artificial setting currently present in and around the car parks.

Through integrating nature, craft, and collective stewardship, the project critiques the displacement of local identity by market-driven urban development, and instead proposes a vision of regenerative architecture rooted in community and care.

Area type : Big Box
- industrial, business and retail areas featuring large buildings, which are usually car based in terms of access and movement;

Area type : Central Seafront
- vibrant architecture associated with seafront leisure; contrast to the orderly Victorian and Edwardian suburbs;

Area type : Primary Centre
- Southend Town Centre; large scale buildings and a variety of comparison shops, services and leisure opportunities;

Area type : Tertiary Centre
- shopping parades with residential areas; most significant historic routes in the Borough; leisure opportunities;

The project looks at ways of reclaiming the stagnant spaces in the area and transforming them into new and dynamic spaces in which the community can begin to give back to the site. While Clarence Road Car Park is serving as an example, the blueprint of the proposal is meant to be applied to any of the neighbouring car parks. The work draws on Agnes Denes' "Wheatfield - A Confrontation" in order to juxtapose agricultural elements into the sterile environment of Southend-on-Sea's High Street. Similar to the Ise Shrine, the character of the building stands in its meaning, idea and tradition, rather than in the construction itself. Therefore, the purpose of the structure is not met when the building is finished, but it rather lies in the process of making, building and replacing, as well as passing on craft from one generation to the next.

egg wrack

barnacles

sand

rocks & seashells

seashells

barnacles

pebbles

sand & pebbles

gutweed

gutweed

gutweed & sand

grass

pitch

concrete aggregate

concrete

pitch & seashells

cracked pitch

concrete aggregate

paint & concrete

bricks

The project began with an analysis of the broader context around Canvey Island. This process materialised through an observational film which depicts the unfiltered character of the area, as well as a series of kinetic models which explore site-specific themes, from the interaction between the layers of natural materials to the movement of the tide and its impact on local activities. These models were then digitally translated into Rhino, further refined and adapted to the needs and conditions of the area, as well as its user groups, with a focus on the young community of the neighbouring Clifftown Theatre Studios. Finally, the structures rearticulate the main drive of the project: the creation of spaces where people can observe, respect and appreciate the natural spatial conditions surrounding them.

Project Images
Community driven spaces for growing, learning and making, with an architecture defined by its material circularity.

101 - 105: Narrative visualisation and material explorations.
106: Physical model composition
107 - 111: Detailed design visualisation and narrative communication

SOUTHEND STAYPORT

PABLO PIMENTEL

As Southend-on-Sea has recently been named a city, its largest piece of infrastructure, London Southend Airport bears the name of a city that sits nearly 60 km away. Southend Stayport seeks to completely retake this piece of Southend from the hands of London holidaymakers directly into the hands of the local Southend community, creating a new urban oasis by reinventing what is often the most polluting and space consuming area of the urban fabric.

The airport perimeter will completely close its doors to the aviation industry and will instead transform itself into Southend's largest park, opening up in all directions to create a democratic, public green space. A map of Essex informs the landscape design, with local flora and fauna creating a new haven for wildlife.

The terminal building, which is served by a train station, is reinvented as the new gateway to this park, becoming Southend Stayport, a large civic building inspired by the old airport's heritage. The old terminal structure is deconstructed, reusing as many elements as possible for minimum environmental impact. These elements are reimagined for the new stayport programme.

The last remaining destinations of the airport, transform alongside the needs of the community, into a new programme, which provides cultural spaces, community gardening and dining, cooperative living and further leisure spaces for all of the Southend Community. This new programme reinvents the vacation, making way for the local staycation, open to all, in the heart of Southend

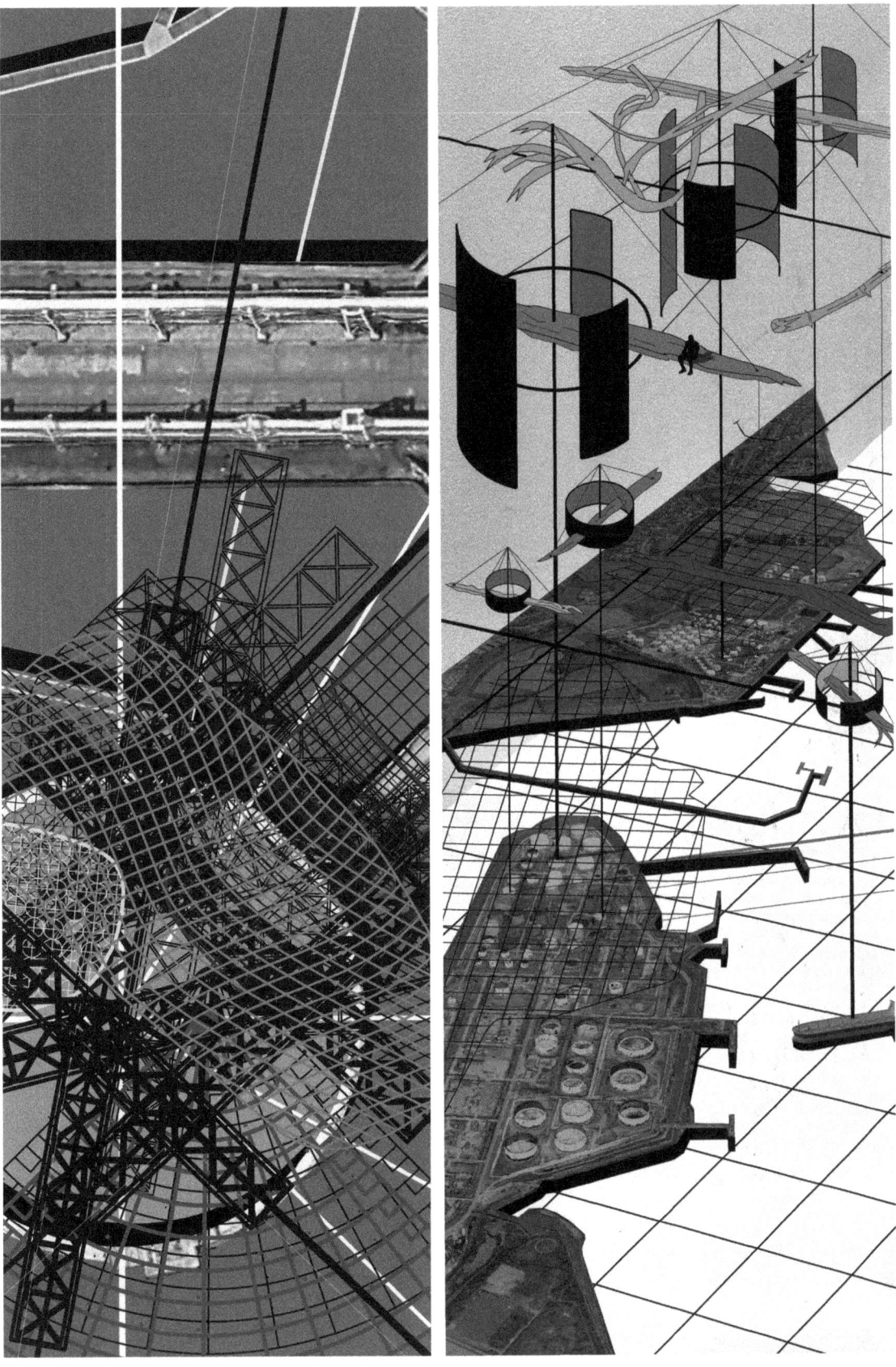

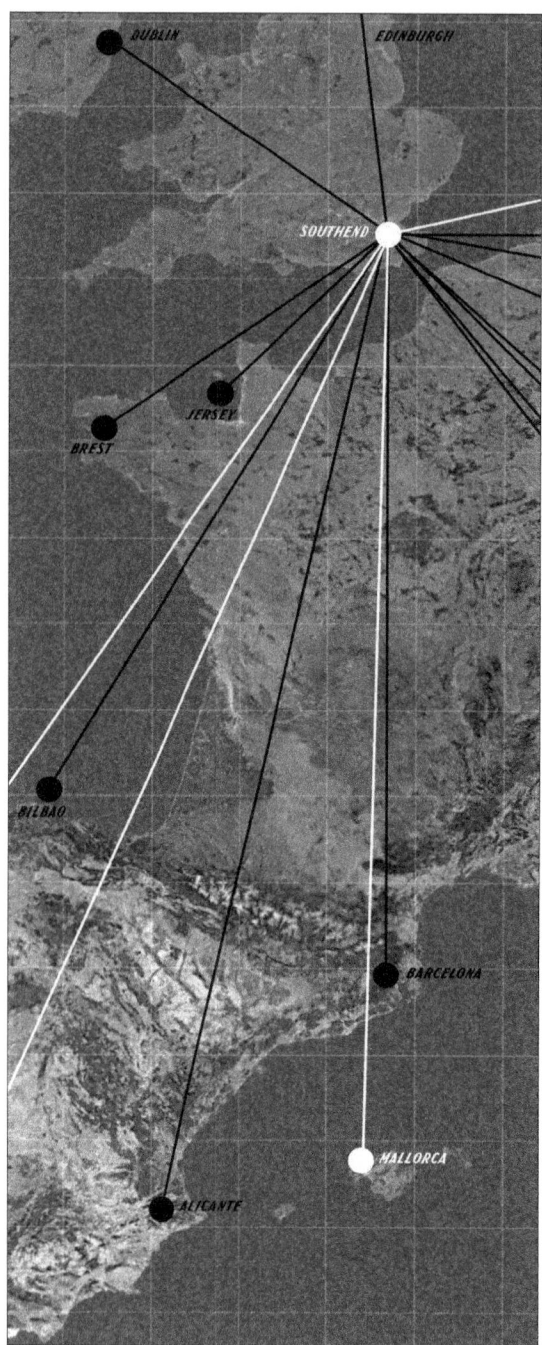
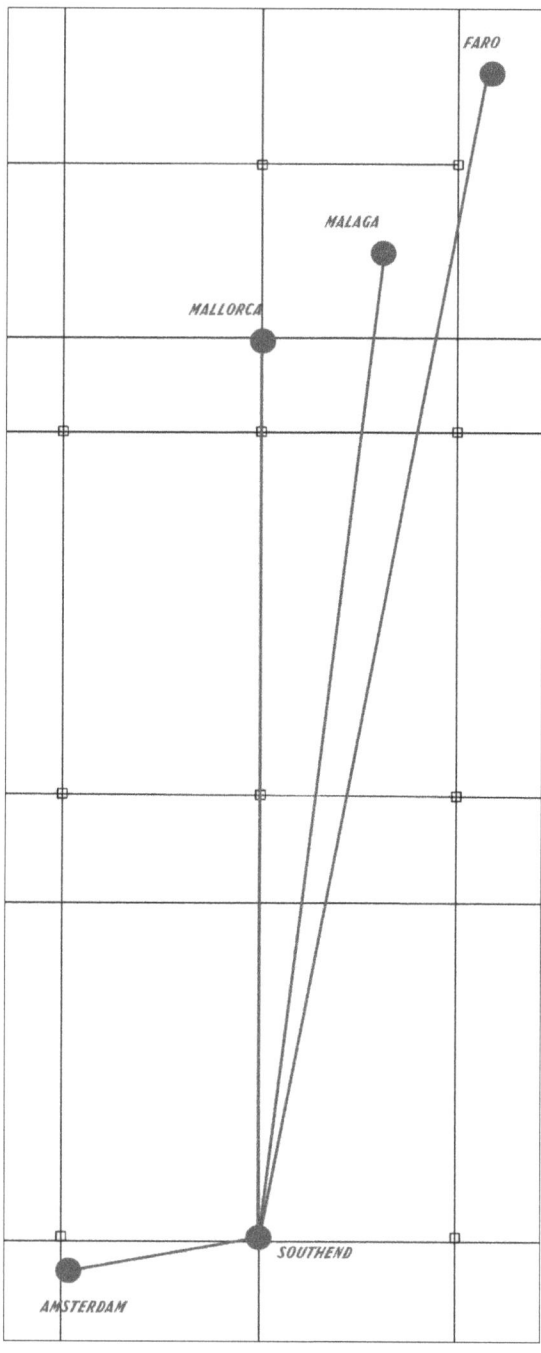

London Southend Airport, which has historically been London's sixth largest airport, is facing an uncertain future as dwindling passenger numbers, a product of the COVID-19 pandemic, have left the airport vacant. At the same time, the government currently seeks to expand other airports like Heathrow by building new runways and terminals, demolishing local villages and upending hundreds of lives.

All these plans spark a debate on the role of airports in the urban realm. Do we sacrifice the welfare of local residents and the fabric of local cities for the benefit of holidaymakers and travellers doing layovers? Do we add more carbon producing industries in a time of climate collapse? Or can a new methodology be created, putting these large pieces of land and infrastructure to a more sustainable and democratic local use.

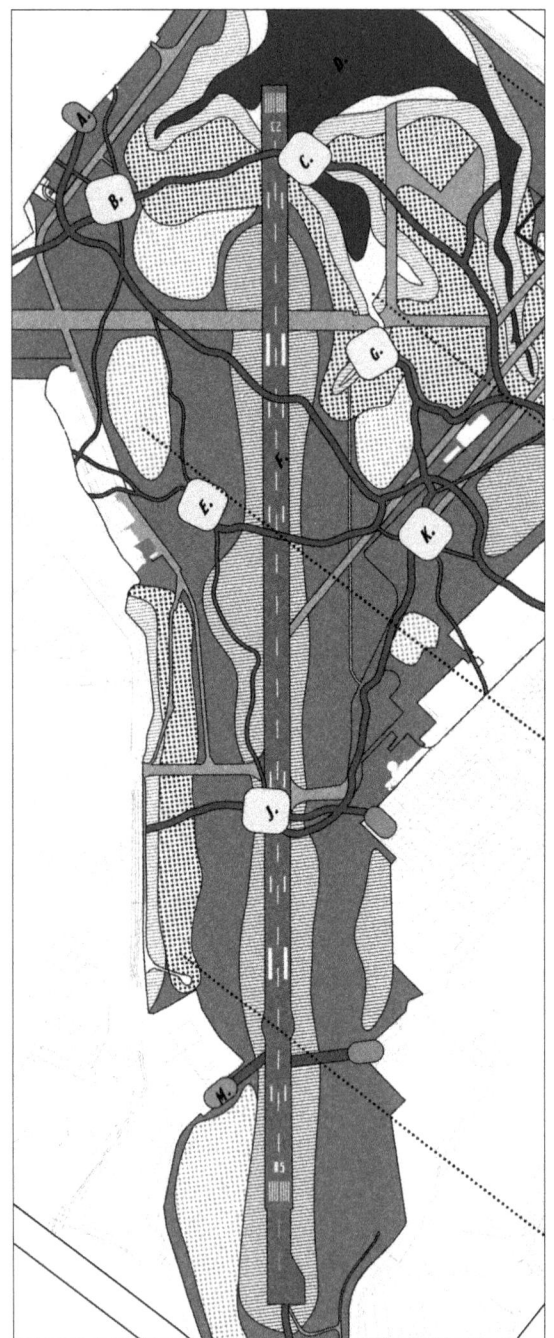 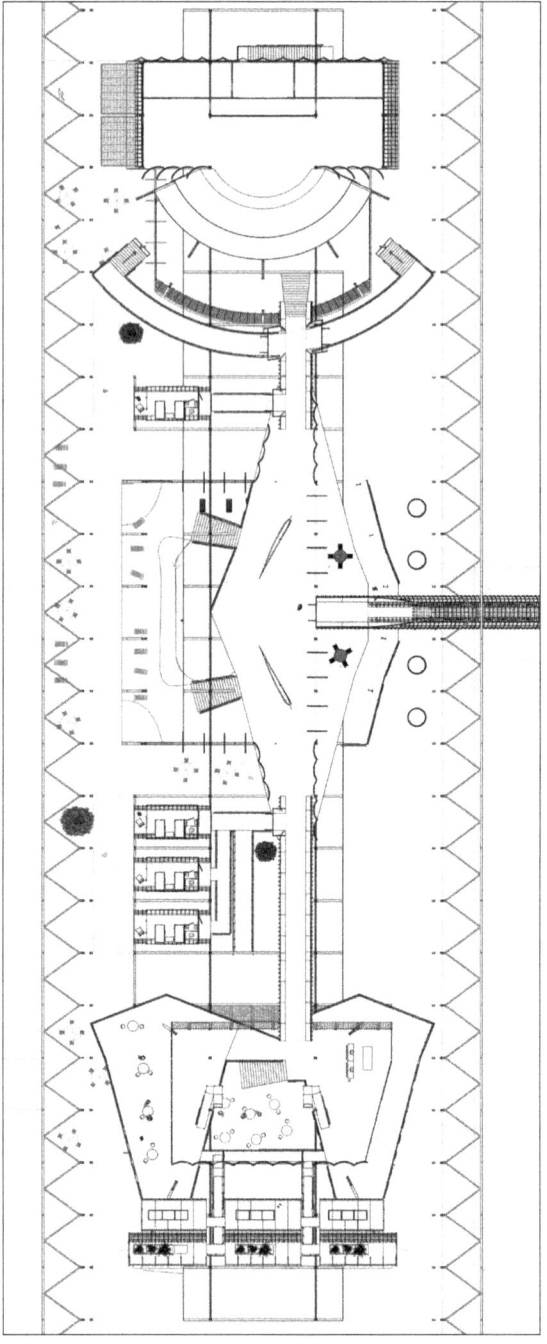

The project evolved through three distinct methodologies: At a masterplan scale, the airport area is transformed into a park planted with local flora and a condensed map of Essex, forming a botanical garden where visitors explore the county's diverse biomes — from marshes and woodlands to wild shrublands. The programme strategy involved reimagining the airport's former destinations as new spaces within the terminal building. These spaces then produced a narrative that guided the project's design methodology. Finally, a holistic circular strategy dictated the reuse of the terminal structure and fragments from the aviation industry. Thousands of aircraft sit abandoned in boneyards around the world, neglected and underused sources of material. A catalogue of elements was created, then assembled and reinvented in line with the needs of the programme.

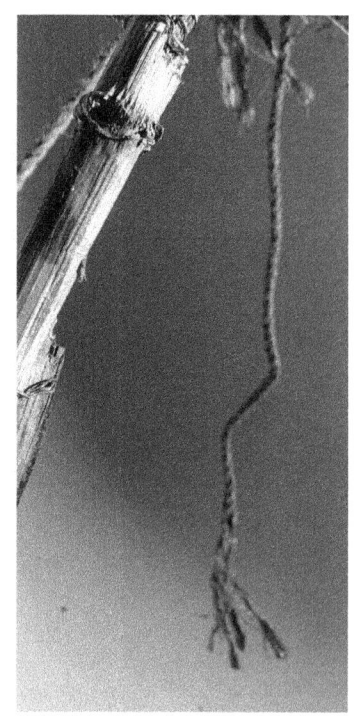

Project Images
An experimental reuse and reinvention of Southend airport, utilising creative structural adaptations to provide spaces for the community of Southend.

113 - 115: Conceptual imagery and contextual framework plots
116 - 117: Architectural development drawings
118 - 119: Conceptual model fragments
120 - 123: Detailed design drawings, models and visualisations.

WINDRUSH CAPITAL

FENN WRIGHT

Windrush Capital is a civic and cultural intervention situated in Tilbury and Grays. The project is designed to embed the narratives and lived experiences of the Windrush generation into the fabric of the town. Recognising the absence of acknowledgment of Caribbean-British contributions in these historically significant arrival points, the project reclaims public space through a series of programmatic interventions rooted in the traditions of Caribbean culture.

The spatial strategy is articulated through three core elements: Memory, Memento, and Music. Memory operates as an archive and oral history forum, a space for intergenerational storytelling and reflection. Memento functions as a curatorial zone, housing objects, documents, and ephemera that symbolise the material culture and migration histories of the community.

Music, meanwhile, engages the urban realm through sound, a performative and participatory space that channels Caribbean traditions as a medium of resistance and celebration.

Windrush Capital is conceived as a spatial framework that enables ongoing cultural activation. Through layered architectural responses, from enclosure and sequencing to soundscaping and material selection, the project challenges dominant narratives of place and belonging. It functions simultaneously as a memorial, community infrastructure, and cultural platform, offering a symbolic redress to historical erasure. Ultimately, it positions architecture as a conduit for restorative justice, foregrounding memory as a catalyst for social regeneration.

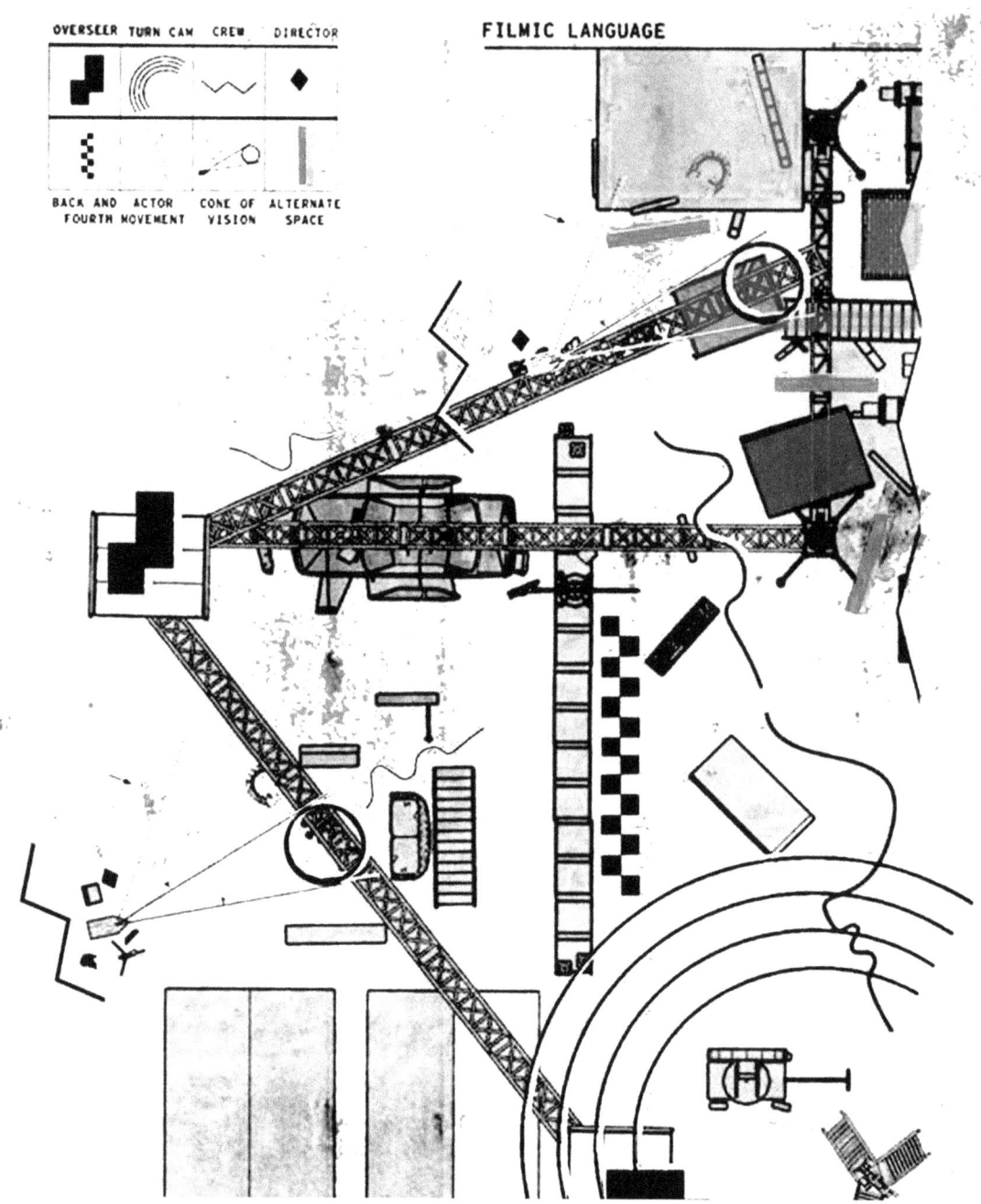

The project is situated in the towns of Tilbury and Grays, a historic point of arrival for Commonwealth citizens in post-war Britain. The Windrush generation, (Caribbean migrants who arrived from 1948) played a pivotal role in rebuilding the nation's public services. However, despite these contributions, they have faced systemic marginalisation, starkly illustrated by the 2018 Windrush Scandal. This narrative is deeply personal. My grandfather, Stanley, was among those whose promise was not kept. Arriving with dreams for a new life, he was left unsupported by the British government. Yet, through resilience he created his own dreamland from what little he had. The project draws upon these personal archives, captured in family photographs and stories, to create an intimate counterpoint to the wider historical narrative. This inform an architectural language that ensured the work remaine rooted in authentic lived experience.

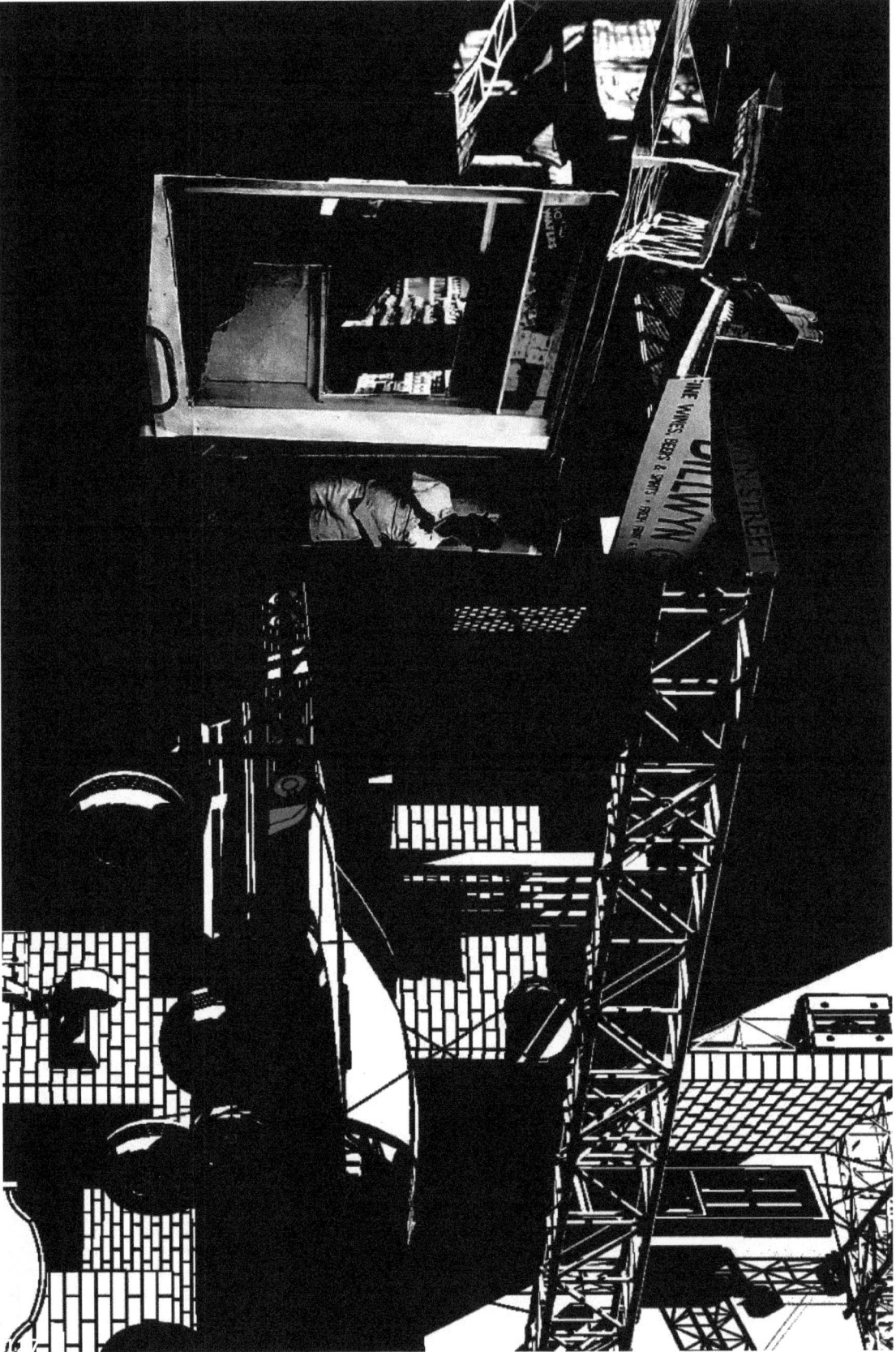

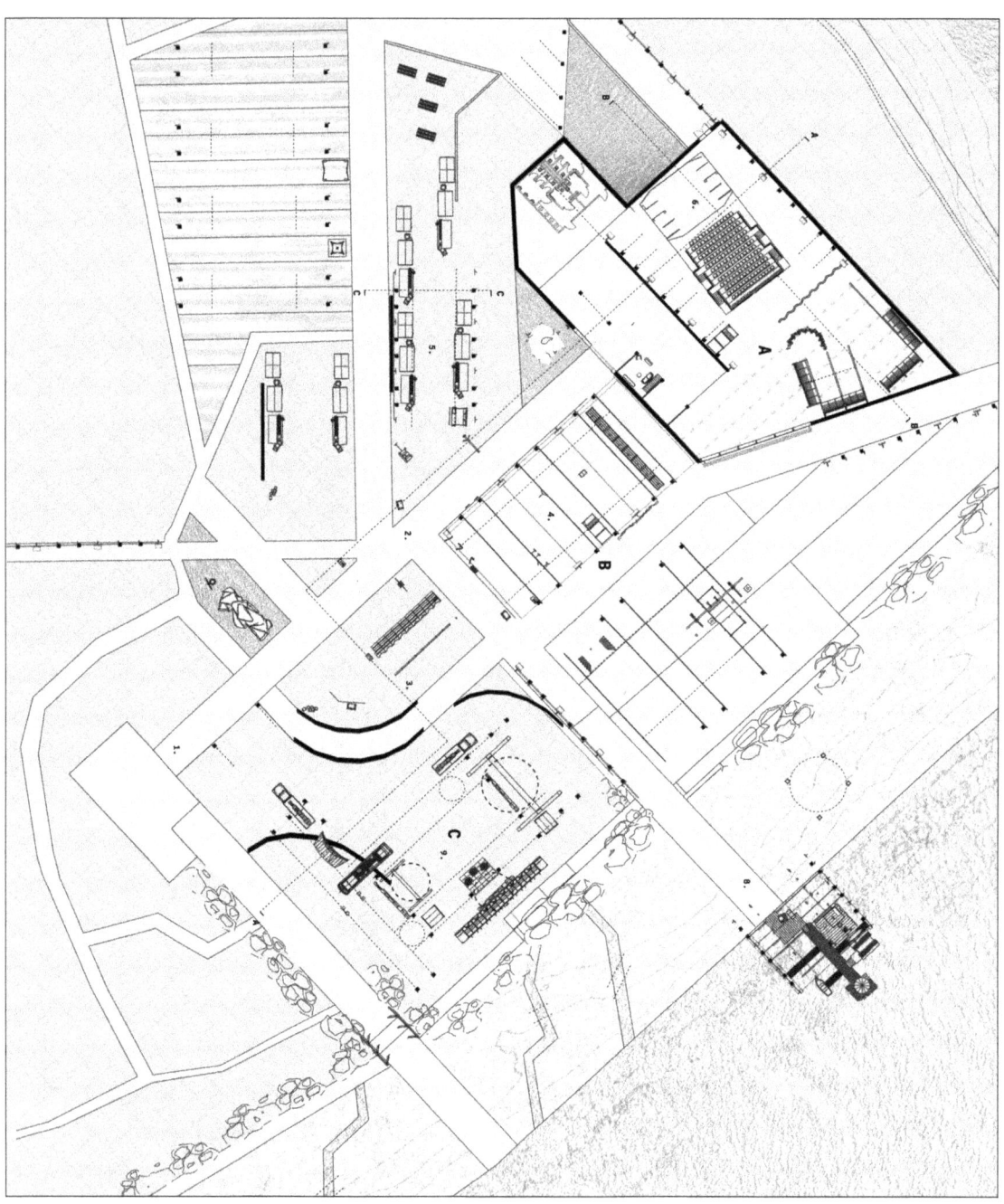

The proposal employs a material and spatial language that reflects diasporic identity and collective memory, creating a visual front door into a culture and time period often overlooked. This spatial narrative invites users to step into the lived histories of the Windrush generation. Central to this approach is the reuse of reclaimed ship parts, directly referencing the vessels that carried many to Britain. Repurposed as structural and sculptural elements, these components act as metaphors for resilience, migration, and transformation, embedding memory within the building fabric. Design exploration focused on threshold conditions, spatial rhythm, and acoustic atmospheres as tools for narrative expression. Rather than a monument, the project establishes an open-ended framework shaped by community input. Flexible programming enables adaptation to festivals, markets, and acts of remembrance, positioning the work as both civic infrastructure and cultural catalyst.

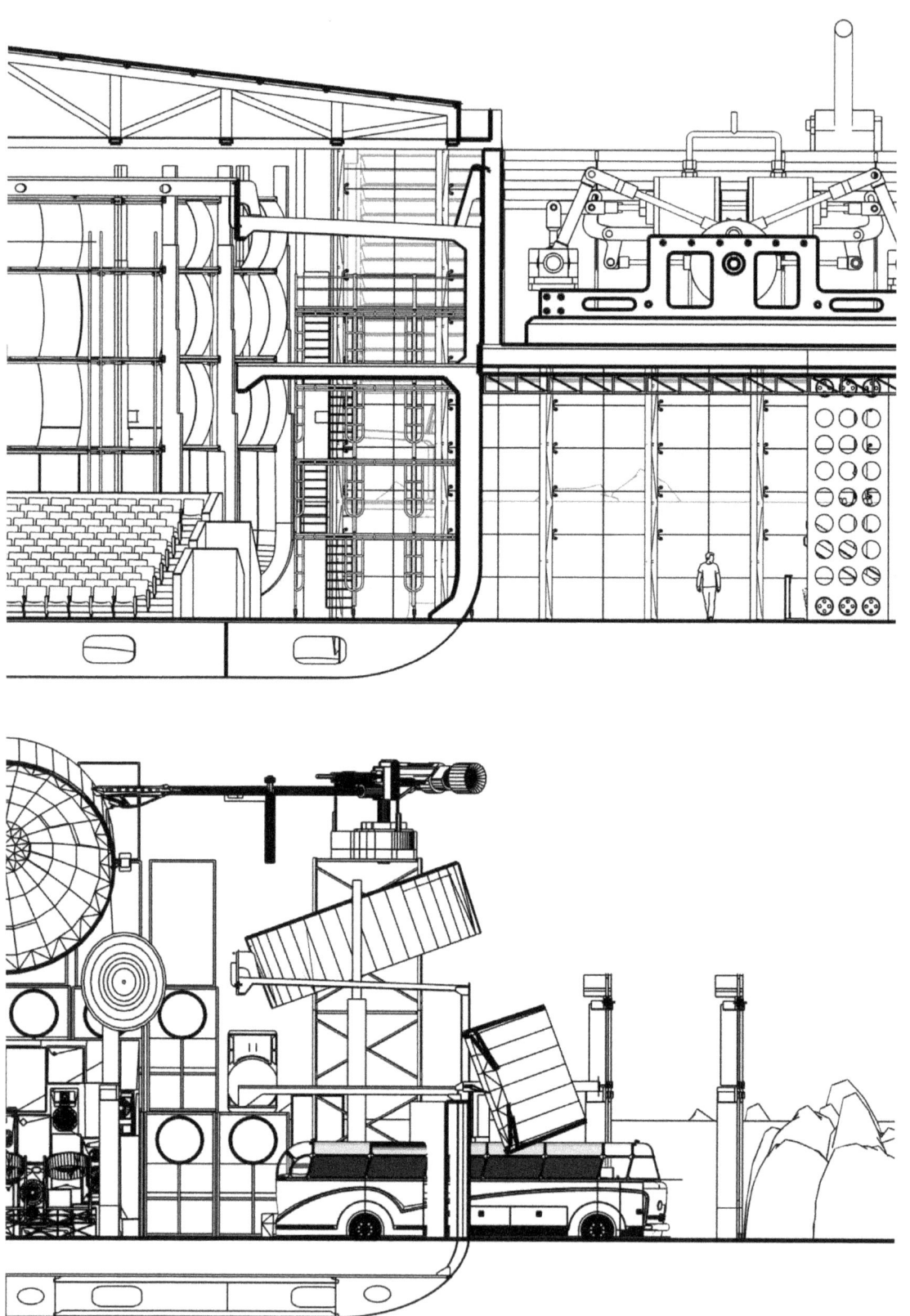

Project Images
Cultural and civic intervention drawing a unique design language from the stories of the Windrush generation.

125 - 127: Conceptual imagery and collages
128 - 130: Architectural development drawings
131 - 135: Design visualisation and narrative communication

Studio 4
Plotting exercises
Hoo Peninsula 2021

Studio 4
Plotting exercises
Canvey Island 2022
East Tilbury 2023

Ioana Zavoianu
Material and details photographs from the fieldtrip to Rotterdam.
Pictured: The Kunsthal by OMA and Rietveld Schröder House
2023 - 2024

Ioana Zavoianu
Church of Grays - Sanctuary of Light and Water
Stills from a short film depicting human moments and a delicate relationship with light within the proposal.
2023 - 2024

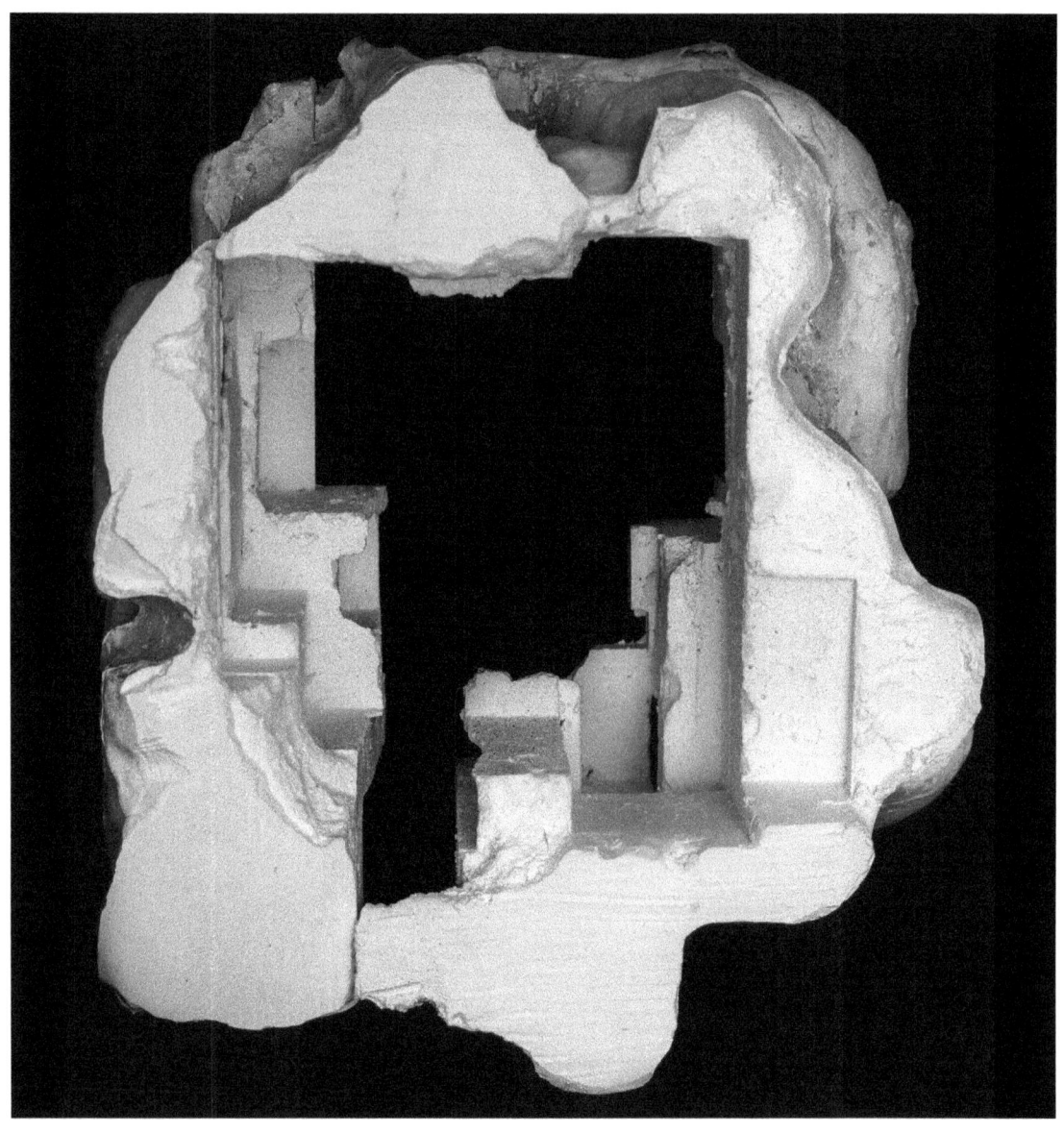

Katarzyna Wojciechowska
Meeting Gravesend
Casting fragments exploring spatial volumes and carvings
2021 - 2022

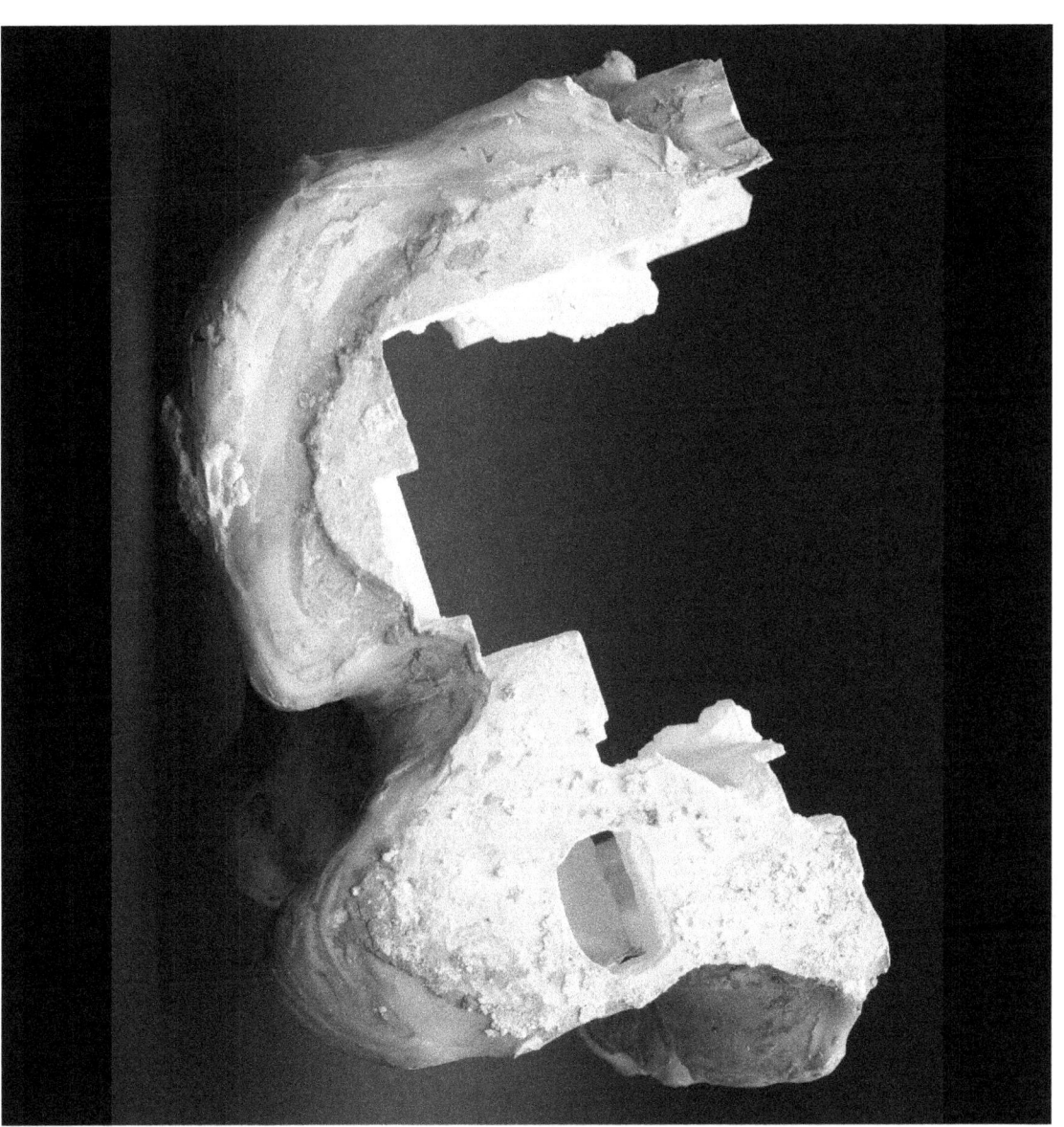

Marta Fernandes Contente
Harmony Amidst Ruins
Experiential model, recomposing fragments and atmospheres
from ruins along the Thames
2023 - 2024

Sofia Rota
Flooding Into The Future
Visualisations exploring human and contextual narratives.
2022 - 2023

Layla El Wadnakssi
Forest School of the Marshes
Model making development from iterative sand casting to detailed timber fragments.
2022 - 2023

Daniel Poshtovenko
Destination Marshland
Conceptual model exploring parasitic typologies within Tilbury
2023 - 2024

Axelle Sibierki
The Ever-Changing Language of Childhood
Eye-level visualisations testing more intimate human moments
within the proposal.
2022 - 2023

Oscar Chainey
The Convent Of Tamesism
Model photographs experimenting with atmospheric lighting to evoke ideas of narrative and myth.
2023 - 2024

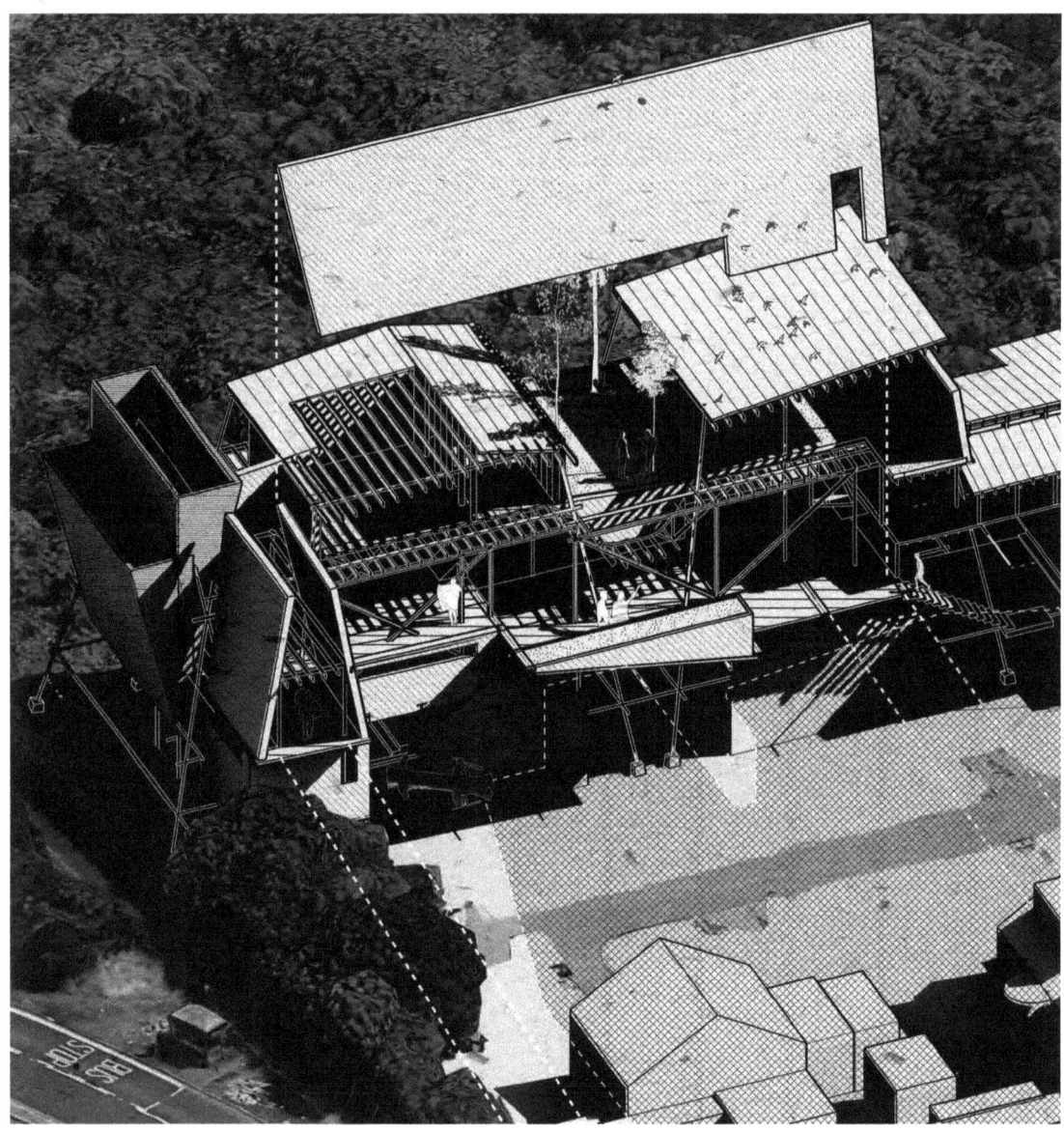

Raoul Tomaselli
Suburbia.test
Conceptual visualisations and collages experimenting with a
floating typology above an existing housing estate.
2022 - 2023

Yuan Padilla
Where the Town Grew Wild
Experimental visualisation testing form and scale for a school in Tilbury.
2023 - 2024

Ray Hung
Windwater Moving Museum
Conceptual storyboards exploring a journey through the proposed museum.
2023 - 2024

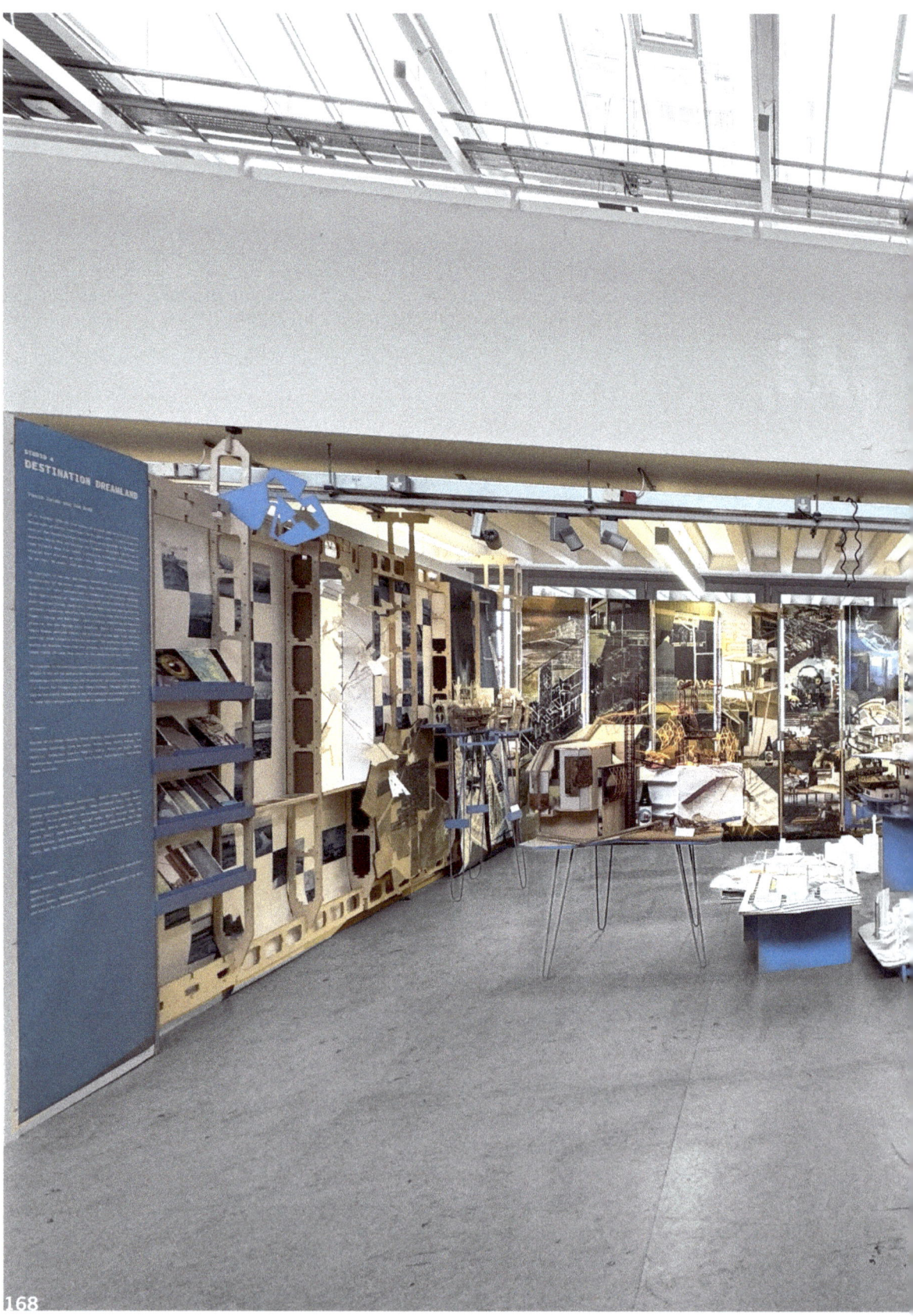

03
SPECULATION

ON SPECULATION

PAOLO ZAIDE & TOM BUDD

One of the most socially progressive housing experiments along the Thames Estuary was the Bata Company Town at East Tilbury, established in the 1920s by the Bata Shoe Company. This planned industrial community combined modernist architectural design with principles from the Garden City movement, offering workers quality affordable homes set within green spaces. Beyond housing, the development included schools, shops, and social amenities, aiming to create a healthy, integrated community that supported not only workers' physical needs but also their education and leisure.

Alongside Bata's visionary project, several Garden Suburbs and planned estates emerged in the region, inspired by similar ideals of improving living conditions outside crowded urban centres. These developments featured low-density housing with private gardens and communal parks, providing residents with more space, light, and fresh air. Designed to counteract the poor sanitation and overcrowding of inner-city areas, these estates reflected a broader movement toward healthier, more humane suburban living for working- and middle-class families along the Thames Estuary.

Both are examples of experiments in future forms of living – one planned, the other a balance with nature. Speculation, for James Corner, is a vital and generative act at the core of landscape architecture and urban design—a deliberate and imaginative practice that transcends mere representation to engage with possibility and invention. Unlike traditional modes of planning or mapping that often seek closure and certainty, speculation opens a field of inquiry that challenges the given, unsettles fixed readings of place, and invites designers to envision alternate futures.

Corner positions speculation as an intellectual and creative operation that destabilizes normative understandings of space and site conditions. It is not speculation for its own sake, nor is it ungrounded fantasy. Rather, it is a disciplined mode of thought—an act of asking *"what if?"* that allows designers to explore latent potentials embedded within ecological processes, social dynamics, and infrastructural networks. Speculation exposes relationships and forces that conventional analyses might overlook, offering a richer, more complex understanding of the site's capacities and constraints.

This speculative impulse is deeply linked to the idea of mapping as a creative agency. In Corner's framework, mapping does not simply chart or represent existing conditions but actively makes new possibilities visible. Speculation fuels this process: by questioning and reframing, it enables the extraction and recombination of elements into novel configurations, inviting alternative narratives and spatial stories. Through speculation, the designer steps beyond documentation into invention, transforming the map into a projective terrain of design exploration.

ACROSS DISCIPLINES:
IMAGINING, DYNAMIC & EVOLVING SYSTEMS

In order to represent a concept that engages with the dynamic, time-based systems that govern the Thames Estuary, equally dynamic and evolving tools and methods are required. The studio looks to embrace emerging digital technologies as a new toolkit for future architects, exploring methods of digital capture, automated production and real time rendering to challenge and strengthen traditional architectural design.

Processes
The rapid influx of AI-based tools is dramatically changing traditional design processes and the studio acts as a testbed to engage, test and critique these new approaches. Adopting radical digital tools into traditional architectural workflows allows for new forms of architectural practice that reflect the rapidly changing industry. Instead of being used to provide generically perfect solutions these tools are challenged and broken with an approach that embraces the inherent mistakes built into these tools to inform novel concepts and architectural oddities.

Provocations
In reaction to these new technologies we ask how digital shifts may change the spaces we inhabit. How will it influence our behaviours of occupation, consumption, work, leisure or those rare moments of simply doing nothing? In the wake of the government's push for technological adoption how does this new digital landscape begin to alter the physical urban environment?

Animation
Due to the dynamic nature of the landscapes along the estuary, the studio adopted a number of time based tools to study, experiment and propose across distinct periods of time. Digital animation, visualisation and filmmaking were key methods adopted to explore how designs may shift and adapt in reaction to rising tides, changing climates and the ongoing spread of development in this area.

Speculation in design isn't about predicting the future or simply crafting desirable outcomes. It's a critical practice that asks *"what if?"*, challenging assumptions and opening new ways of thinking about technology, society, and culture. Rather than solving problems, speculative design provokes reflection and dialogue. The design methods in this section propose a radical rethink of how environments are traditionally conceptualised, represented, and engaged, embracing potential for large-scale change across time and place. They move fluidly between emerging digital environments and intuitive, hands-on experimentation within physical contexts. *Speculation* functions as a means of exploring possibilities over predictions. It repositions design as a cultural and imaginative act, less about function, more about enabling collective social dreaming and imagining dynamic, evolving alternative futures.

CYBERPLACE IN THE METAVERSE

BODHI HORTON

CAN OUR CONCEPTIONS OF PLACE EXIST WITHIN THE METAVERSE?

The metaverse, promised as a seamless integration of our physical and digital realities, captured mass attention with visions of virtual communities, economies, and personalised spaces.[01] Projects like Decentraland, a blockchain-based world launched in 2020, aimed to create decentralised hubs for social and economic life.[02] Yet, after years of hype and investment, the discourse around virtual worlds seems to have lost its relevance and publicity. Perhaps the architects of the metaverse have finally confronted a fundamental suspicion: that there is no place like a real place.

This essay argues that our conceptions of 'place' can indeed exist within virtual worlds, but that current iterations fail because they are built on a flawed understanding of what constitutes a place. They pursue an abstract, disembodied model of 'cyberspace' rather than an experiential, contextual 'cyberplace'. True virtual place-making is not merely a technological challenge of sensory stimulation but a philosophical and structural one. To succeed, the metaverse must (1) overcome the flawed 'cyberspace' paradigm by prioritising context over discrete objects, (2) establish the conditions for place through genuine embodiment and coherent sensory experience, and (3) build social and economic structures that incentivise collaborative placemaking over financial speculation. The question, then, is whether projects like Decentraland can offer a meaningful alternative, or whether they remain little more than loosely connected expanses of placelessness.

THE 'CYBERSPACE' PARADIGM

The primary obstacle preventing the metaverse from fostering a sense of place is its conceptual foundation as 'cyberspace'. This term, popularised by William Gibson in his 1984 novel Neuromancer, described a "consensual hallucination experienced daily by billions... a graphic representation of data abstracted from the banks of every computer in the human system."[03] This literary origin is crucial; it defined the virtual realm not as a parallel reality to be inhabited, but as a visualisation of abstract information, a landscape of pure data, disregarding the human labour and the vast physical servers that maintain this digital world. This foundational idea of a disembodied, informational reality has profoundly shaped the technological and philosophical approach to building virtual worlds. The paradigm views the virtual realm not as a built environment to be inhabited, but as a commodity to be conquered and traversed. This world view is revealed through two dominant metaphors that stem directly from this origin: the path and the frontier.

The 'path metaphor' conceives of virtual reality as a series of nodes or landmarks connected by trajectories. The user is positioned as an external observer travelling along a predetermined route, moving from one point to the next. This model finds its roots in early internet navigation, the hyperlink, and has been cemented by decades of video game design that relies on waypoints, mission markers, and fast travel systems. These mechanics reduce the environment to a problem of navigation. Space becomes a utility to be overcome in order to reach a destination, rather than a medium to be experienced. This creates a detached impression of a world seen from afar, where objects exist in front of a void rather than within a cohesive background. Like traditional science studying objects decontextualised from their settings, this model privileges individual figures over their ground. However, as geographer Yi-Fu Tuan argues, we do not experience our world as abstract 'space,' a geometric expanse of coordinates, but as 'place', which is space endowed with human meaning and value.[04] Places are not mere destinations but immersive contexts that envelop us. The path metaphor, by reducing the environment to a network, keeps the virtual world perpetually in the realm of abstract space, producing a sterile and un-situated experience.

Complementing this is the 'frontier metaphor', a product of colonial mythology that frames cyberspace as a vast, empty territory awaiting claim and settlement. This perspective, deeply embedded in Silicon Valley's techno-libertarian ideology, treats space as a raw commodity. It echoes the rhetoric of American Manifest Destiny, casting developers and users as pioneers taming a digital wilderness. John Perry Barlow's 1996 "A Declaration of the Independence of Cyberspace" famously articulated this ethos, declaring the virtual world a new, sovereign space "not subject to your laws," a realm free from the "tyrannies" of physical government and material constraint.[05] While this rhetoric is powerful and has fuelled immense investment and innovation, it is built on a dangerous fallacy. The 'frontier' was never truly empty; its settlement involved the displacement of existing cultures and the imposition of a new order. Similarly, cyberspace is not an empty void, it was built as a social network, and treating it as a raw resource to be claimed promotes a culture of extraction and speculation over one of stewardship and cultivation.

MARKETING IMAGES OF THE PICTURESQUE

The rush to acquire and own digital territory becomes the primary activity. The nature of the 'environment' being claimed is simply a collection of identifiable codes; if the world is merely a network of nodes, as the path metaphor suggests, then the frontier exists only as an investment strategy, not as a tangible environment to be encountered and shaped.

Together, these metaphors construct a transcendent vision of cyberspace that is inherently placeless. The focus on data, paths, and acquisition creates a world optimised for disembodied observation and economic transaction, not embodied inhabitation. Gibson's vision was of minds jacked into the Matrix, leaving the body behind. This split between mind and body, information and environment, lies at the heart of the cyberspace paradigm's failure. Without a persistent, meaningful background that grounds the user, without the possibility of containment, and without the encouragement of non-linear, serendipitous exploration, the user cannot be truly situated. Their experience is reduced to navigating a schematic or managing a portfolio. To move forward, we must reject this paradigm and its flawed metaphors. We must rethink the virtual world not as 'cyberspace' but as 'cyberplace'.

EMBODIMENT AND CONTEXT

The transition from abstract cyberspace to experiential cyberplace requires a new ontological ground, a meaningful, shared space with real experiences and relationships. It necessitates a philosophical shift away from the dualism inherent in the cyberspace paradigm towards an understanding of being in the world. It requires moving from viewing the virtual world as a set of locations to be observed to an environment in which one can be embedded. Drawing on phenomenological thought, particularly the work of Maurice Merleau-Ponty, two conditions are paramount for this transition: embodiment and context.

First, and most fundamentally, place requires embodiment, the sensation of having a physical presence within the world. For Merleau-Ponty, our body is not merely an object among other objects; it is the very vehicle of our being in the world, the centre from which all perception and experience radiates.[06] Our perception is not a detached intellectual exercise but a bodily engagement with our surroundings. To recognise ourselves in a cyberplace, we must feel situated within a virtual body, a 'figure' that can sense, perceive, and act upon its environment. This means more than just customising a visual avatar. It requires the establishment of a coherent body schema, our unconscious, intuitive sense of our body's position, boundaries, and capabilities. A successful virtual embodiment occurs when the virtual body's actions align seamlessly with our intentions, when its sensory feedback is predictable and consistent. When we reach for a virtual object, our hand should move as expected, and the object should react according to consistent physics. This creates a functional presence that allows the virtual body to feel like an extension of our own sense of the body, rather than a puppet we are remotely controlling. The common phenomenon of the "uncanny valley", where avatars' hyper-realistic appearance is coupled with unnatural movement, demonstrates this principle; the break in the body schema shatters the sense of presence far more than simplified graphics ever could.

Second, this embodied figure must exist within a meaningful context. Merleau-Ponty's concept of the "wedding of figure to ground" is crucial here. For a place to be perceived, the background cannot be a black void, a static skybox, or an irrelevant backdrop; it must be an

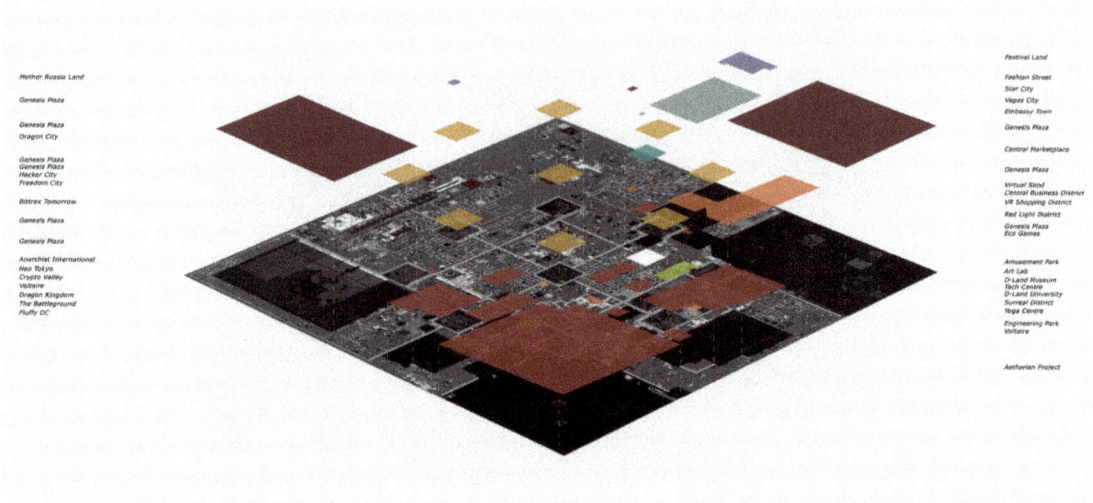

active, integral part of the experience. The ground gives the figure its meaning and situation. This idea is echoed in the architectural theory of Christian Norberg-Schulz, who posited the concept of genius loci, or the "spirit of a place."[07] A place, for Norberg-Schulz, is a totality, a distinct character that arises from the holistic interplay of its built forms, its natural environment, and the human life that unfolds within it.[08] To create a cyberplace with a true genius loci, its world must possess a coherent 'materiality' and structure that allows for embeddedness. Whether the virtual world represents a real city or a fantastical realm, its internal logic, its physics, its lighting, its atmospheric conditions, its ambient sounds must be consistent and enveloping. The environment must feel persistent and consequential, a shared ground that makes coexistence possible and allows the social and personal meanings that constitute 'place' to form. Freedom, in this phenomenological view, comes not from the rootless transcendence promised by cyberspace but from the recognition and inhabitation of a meaningful context.

Achieving this technologically is a nuanced challenge. The immediate impulse is to chase photorealism with ever more powerful hardware: haptic suits, omnidirectional treadmills, and olfactory simulators that can stimulate our senses. However, the goal should not be sensory overload or mere visual fidelity. An excess of competing, uncoordinated stimuli can lead to a distracted and disjointed experience, undermining the very immersion it seeks to create. As theorists of the attention economy note, when information is bountiful, attention becomes scarce. A cacophony of high-fidelity but incoherent sensory data scatters our attention and prevents us from settling into the experience. Thus, the fundamental quality for creating cyberplace is not hyper-realism but naturalness, a term that here means coherence and intuitive responsiveness. A virtual environment that stimulates our senses in a holistic way that mirrors the logic of our physical world perception will feel more immersive than a photorealistic but sensorially chaotic one. The human brain is exceptionally good at suspending disbelief and filling in perceptual gaps, but only if the core experiential framework is sound. A world with simpler graphics but with perfectly synchronised audio, responsive physics, and consistent environmental cues allows the user to forgive visual imperfections and become absorbed, because their embodiment within the context feels authentic and whole.

THE ARCHITECTURAL FLAWS OF DECENTRALAND

Decentraland serves as a compelling case study of how a virtual world, despite its ambitions for a user-created utopia, can fail to achieve 'place' by violating these core principles of embodiment and context. Its failure is not merely aesthetic or the result of immature technology, but is deeply architectural, rooted in flawed systems of authorship and economics that actively prevent the emergence of a cohesive cyberplace. It is a world built firmly on the 'cyberspace' paradigm.

Fragmented Authorship and the Absence of Context: Decentraland promotes a model of user authorship where individuals purchase a non-fungible LAND token, a 16 x 16 metre plot on a fixed grid, on which they can build anything.[09] In theory, this democratises creation. In practice, it generates a fragmented and incoherent landscape defined by protocols and exceptions rather than integrated design. The "sandbox" model, lacking any shared aesthetic, zoning principles, or collaborative infrastructure, encourages the creation of isolated objects rather than

integrated contexts. Visiting Decentraland is an experience of traversing a monotonous, algorithmically generated terrain sporadically dotted with disconnected constructions: a garish, flashing casino stands next to a low-effort cube, which sits beside a completely empty plot, which in turn borders a pixelated reproduction of a meme. There is no holistic sense of a world, only a collection of individual projects that fail to form a meaningful whole.

This design epitomises the 'cyberspace' paradigm. The world is a literal grid, a schematic of property rights. The experience is one of moving between nodes (the authored plots) across an otherwise empty and meaningless background, connected by perfunctory paths that resemble a circuit board on the map more than meaningful trajectories. It is the architectural equivalent of a webpage full of disconnected hyperlinks. There is no genius loci. The context is invisible, and a sense of situatedness can only be gleaned from looking at the 2D map, not from experiencing the 3D environment. This stands in stark contrast to the principles of successful urban planning articulated by thinkers like Jane Jacobs, who championed the organic complexity of cities, the mixture of uses, the importance of public spaces, and the "sidewalk ballet" that creates a sense of community and safety.[10] Decentraland's rigid grid and lack of shared civic spaces actively preclude this kind of organic, placemaking activity.

Speculative Economics over Place-Making:
The world's economy is another significant barrier. To participate in a meaningful way, users must purchase MANA, a cryptocurrency, to buy LAND.[11] This structure, from its inception, has made Decentraland primarily a vehicle for high-risk financial investment, a "digital gold rush" that perfectly illustrates the frontier metaphor.[12] The value of a plot is driven not by the quality of the experience it offers, the beauty of its design, or its contribution to the community, but by external factors like the volatility of the cryptocurrency market, its proximity to a developer-built hub, or pure speculation. Consequently, the intention behind many constructions is not to contribute to a shared world but to act as a placeholder for an asset, often manifested as a virtual billboard or a simple structure designed to attract traffic for advertising revenue.

This economic model incentivises speculation over genuine placemaking, attracting investors rather than community builders, residents, and artisans. When a single plot of digital land can trade for thousands or even millions of real-world dollars, the pressure to monetise overwhelms any impulse to create non-commercial, communal, or purely aesthetic spaces. One is unlikely to build a public park or a quiet library on an asset that represents a significant financial investment demanding a return. The very value of Decentraland is therefore divorced from its quality as a place. This economic architecture ensures that the world develops not according to human needs for community and belonging, but according to the cold logic of capital investment, resulting in a landscape littered with financial instruments rather than inhabited places.

Contradictory and Centralised Governance:
Finally, the project's foundational claim of decentralisation is undermined by its actual governance structure. Decentraland operates as a Decentralised Autonomous Organisation (DAO), where LAND and MANA holders can vote on policy proposals.[13] However, voting power is proportional to the amount of LAND or wrapped MANA owned, a plutocratic system that grants the wealthiest users the most control.[14] This is not a digital democracy, but a shareholder meeting. Furthermore, this system is ultimately subordinate to a centralised Security Advisory Board (SAB)

created by the original founders. This five-member board has the power to upgrade smart contracts, blacklist assets, and even halt the entire platform, effectively overriding any community vote in the name of security.

This contradiction between the marketing narrative of decentralisation and the reality of a plutocratic and centrally controlled system creates a fundamental inauthenticity. This centralisation is physically manifest in the landscape itself, where grand, professionally designed plazas and district centres, built by the developers, monopolise the map and serve as the true landmarks and traffic hubs. These zones, while more visually coherent, stand in stark opposition to the ethos of a user-generated world, highlighting the failure of the distributed model to produce compelling public spaces on its own. In essence, Decentraland reflects the ideals of a decentralised place but fails to create the experience of one. Its core architecture produces a fragmented, placeless cyberspace defined by a cryptocurrency craze and a contradictory governance model, not a genuine desire to foster an embodied virtual community.

CONCLUSION

Our conceptions of place can exist in the metaverse, but this potential is far from being realised. The capacity to feel present, to form attachments to a location, and to build community within a shared context is a fundamental part of the human condition that is not tethered exclusively to the physical world. However, as this analysis has shown, the challenge is less technological than it is philosophical and structural. The prevailing 'cyberspace' model, with its emphasis on paths, frontiers, and decontextualised objects, is fundamentally incapable of fostering the deep, situated experience that defines 'place'. It is a paradigm of disembodiment, abstraction, and instrumentalism.

The creation of a true 'cyberplace' depends on a radical shift in approach. It requires establishing the conditions for embodiment and context, where users feel a genuine bodily presence within a coherent, meaningful environment that envelops and grounds them. This means building worlds where the background matters as much as the figure, and where a consistent and intuitive logic, a genius loci, governs the experience. Technology must serve this goal by aiming for naturalness and sensory harmony, prioritising holistic coherence over disjointed hyperrealism or spectacle.

The failure of a project like Decentraland is instructive. Its fragmented landscape, speculative economy, and contradictory governance reveal that even with the ideal of user authorship, a world built on flawed architectural principles will fail to become a place. It demonstrates that simply handing users tools on a grid is not enough; a framework for collaborative context building is essential. The core issue moving forward is therefore one of authorial intent. Who is building these virtual worlds, and for what purpose? Are they designed as platforms for financial speculation, as centrally controlled theme parks masquerading as open worlds, or as genuine frameworks for the collaborative creation of community and meaning? Until the architects of the metaverse prioritise the human experience of being in a world over the abstract logic of owning a piece of it, their creations will remain empty frontiers rather than places we can call home.

Notes

(01) Interaction Design Foundation, *What Is the Metaverse?* https://www.interaction-design.org/literature/topics/metaverse.

(02) Cryptopedia Staff, "Decentraland (MANA): A Virtual World Built on Ethereum," *Cryptopedia* (Gemini), updated November 1, 2023, https://www.gemini.com/en-US/cryptopedia/decentraland-defi-ethereum-based.

(03) Jeremy M. Norman, "'Cyberspace' Popularized," *History of Information,* 1984, https://www.historyofinformation.com/detail.php?id=983.

(04) Yi-Fu Tuan, Space and Place: The Perspective of Experience (Minneapolis: University of Minnesota Press, 1977)

(05) John Perry Barlow, *"A Declaration of the Independence of Cyberspace," Diplo Resource, 1996*, https://www.diplomacy.edu/resource/a-declaration-of-the-independence-of-cyberspace/.

(06) "The Phenomenology of Merleau-Ponty and Embodiment in the World," *Aeon Essays*

(07) Università per Stranieri di Perugia, "Genius Loci," https://www.unistrapg.it/it/genius-loci.

(08) Akkelies van Nes, "The Heaven, the Earth and the Optic Array," *TU Delft OPEN Journals*, 2008

(09) Decentraland Documentation, "Decentraland: Publishing Options," updated November 1, 2023, https://docs.decentraland.org/creator/development-guide/sdk7/publishing-permissions/.

(10) Jane Jacobs, *The Death and Life of Great American Cities* (New York: Random House, 1961).

(11) Decentraland, "What Is Decentraland?," *Decentraland Whitepaper,* https://decentraland.org/whitepaper.pdf

(12) Hyscaler, "2024 Metaverse Economy: Gold Rush Insights," https://hyscaler.com/insights/2024-metaverse-economy-gold-rush-insights/.

(13) 'Decentraland (DCL) Metaverse: Explained - Ledger'.

(14) 'DAO User Guide't ex

TOMORROW'S IMAGE FACTORIES

ERIC TURNER

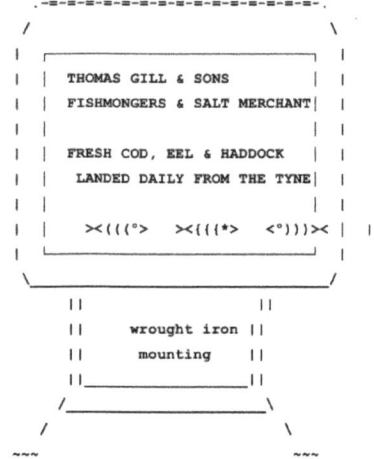

ASCII art of a tyneside fishmonger's sign, ChatGPT-4o

During the tail-end of the industrial revolution in the late nineteenth century, British poet and writer William Morris published a series of essays looking onward towards the next major shift in labour, titled 'A Factory as It May Be'. A speculative account of the factories of the future, Morris posits an acceleration of mechanisation and automation within these factories as a step towards an equitable, socialist society. The work schedule of a factory worker as well as the programme and ornament of the factory itself are described, where workers are now artisans whose labour is only required for four hours a day.[01] The factories become beautifully ornamented spaces serving their community, providing education and dining for all. Alas these projections have turned out to bear little resemblance to contemporary work culture - in the UK, mechanical automata have indeed accelerated through manufacturing and logistics workplaces, but this has merely resulted in a general displacement of the workforce, shifting from manual labour to computer-facing labour.

Unlike the factory workers of Morris's time and the machinery that automated their labour, today's white-collar workforce is afforded total exposure to and interaction with its inevitable future automator, generative AI. It is perhaps a cruel preview for today's worker to use AI in banal and recreational ways (a recent example is the OpenAI *Studio Ghibli* style image filter, swiftly appropriated by all cliques of the internet from meme culture to fascist propaganda) with the underlying knowledge that these technologies are being refined through their participation. Refined to automate most, if not all, of the labour that they produce in exchange for a living; it is apparent that Morris's socialist utopia is again unlikely to manifest as a result of this second great shift in work culture, but with a rapidly increasing amount of labour becoming possible to automate, a new type of coexistence with these AI technologies is seemingly inevitable. How will we collaborate and co-produce with these alternate intelligences, and how will they create shifts in our cities, landscapes and imagination?

A PALACE OF INDUSTRY: A SPECULATIVE PRECEDENT

The manufacturing of vessels in shipyards comprised one of Britain's largest industries during Morris's writing of *A Factory as It May Be*, a laborious and dangerous manual process, yet comparably so favourable to unemployment that the shipbuilder's unions largely resisted mechanisation for a number of decades.[02] Morris, instead, put forward a compromise; more favourable working conditions for factory workers enabled by automation rather than hampered by it - an equitable coexistence with automata that would be made possible by systemic economic and political change to ensure labour is not displaced. He also, crucially, challenges the urbanism that was emerging as a result of industry within the existing social system. A shipbuilder working on the Tyne or in London's Docklands would have lived close and commuted by foot to the shipyard, always within the clutches of the yard's grime, noise and visual presence. Commutes function as integral threads through the cityscape, necessitated by work and therefore an extension of the architectural space of labour; a shifting free market of street vendors and brick and mortar shops punctuate this thread. The commute is the midpoint of the labourer's typical spatial sequence: not home yet not working. Envisioned by Morris is an inversion of this spatial sequence in which the factory acts as a trivial median point between more important acts of living, education, dining, craftsmanship and entertainment: time is made for these other acts through automation. 'Nightmare buildings', as he refers to the nineteenth century factory, 'typify the work they are built for, and lack what they are, temples of overcrowding and adulteration [...] so it is not difficult to think of our factory buildings showing on their outsides what they are for, reasonable and light work, cheered at every step by hope and pleasure'. Morris is clear that labour, its architecture and its urbanism are reciprocal entities - humane work practices and humane design reinforce one another within an urban system, the urbanism of labour comprising a network of these interrelated nodes woven together through the individually distinct threads of the commute.

Four decades on from *A Factory as it May Be*, Adolf Loos also drew parallels between labour and ornament, short-sightedly equating an increase in ornament on an object or building with an increase in labour time and therefore price.[03] Automation and mass manufacturing reduce this to a moot point as machine time in producing an ornamented item bears a much different relation to costs and energy compared to human time. In fact, after Loos's time, finely crafted 'perfect' austere minimalism entered the mainstream as a popular design language - more value, in this case, is assigned to a hand-fabricated minimal Loosian object than a mass-manufactured ornamental one. Clearly today we still place value in material and in human craft over merely the quantity of labour that something takes to be created.

This value we place in craft applies also to architectural and urban scales. Beyond manual and traditionally automated labour, how will artificial labour disrupt our cities?

'Our factory which is externally beautiful will not be inside like a clean jail or workhouse; the architecture will come inside in the form of such ornament as may be suitable to the special circumstances. Nor can I see why the highest and most intellectual art, pictures, sculpture, and the like should not adorn a true palace of industry.'[1]

CITIES & LABOUR

Little has changed when reading the contemporary city through the lens of labour. Urban sprawl and changes in land value have dispersed these nodes and overall lengthened the threads that we follow as our commutes. But the sequence of architectures that we experience travelling between workplace, home and tertiary activity remain, in concept, the same as what Morris observed and reacted to in the 19th century.

A disruptor to our established urban sequencing in recent memory is the 2020 coronavirus pandemic. It served (as the seepage of AI technologies into our day-to-day is now serving) as a preview of a widespread readjustment to work culture and our urban environment. Locked-down cities retained their nodal arrangement but the binding agent, the commute, for a huge number of people disappeared completely. The first wave of openly accessible AI tools emerged in this same era, positioning the coronavirus pandemic as an incubator - we emerged from lockdown simultaneously with our new alternate intelligences to a new world paradigm for work, design and thought.

What seems to exist currently is a hybrid system in which AI is used in lieu of human labour to realise a human intent. In the workplace, AI assistants draft emails and generate imagery. Shifts to views and vistas (nodes) on our commute come in the form of evolving signage, once upon a time painted, then digitally collaged, now generated with a string of text and a click. There is still an intangible feeling that such an email, or image, is artificial. But this rise in artifice that has materialised in the real world is read and absorbed by the subconscious. We are confronted at every node of our day (at work, on our commute, during leisure, on the internet at home) with proof that activities that we believed were distinctly human are achievable without the human hand. This sense of uselessness at a city's scale will be ruinous for culture - therefore authorship of our cities must lie firmly in our hands. We must negotiate around the inevitability of this by inserting ourselves into the process, collaborating and co-producing with our alternate intelligences.

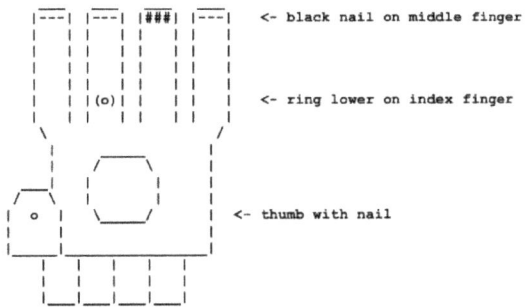

ASCII art based on description of author's hand, ChatGPT-4o

THE HAND

The 'human touch' is tricky to define - simply the presence of imperfection often summons an endearing feeling of connection and relatability. The 'aesthetics' of AI (it is debatable if this exists - an average of data is not a distinct thing) can also be characterised by a different type of (nowadays diminishing) imperfection. Seemingly we only value these imperfections when they tell us a story of human thought processes; the process with which AI arrives at a conclusion is algorithmic, cyclical and thoughtless - it follows a linear prompt-to-output process of echo-chambered self-critique through revisions.

Therefore imperfections are often confusing, unsettling, difficult to resolve. I have sought to experiment with methods and processes which blur the traditional boundaries of authorship in my design work. In automating the instinct of my own hand through AI and entering into an iterative back-and-forth process between it and myself, a new form of tense composite between human and artificial is created, visually energetic and ready to break apart at any moment. It is rare that the analogue and artificial instincts are convergent - they often exist in opposition to one another.

As a rule, all artificial intelligence models that have emerged thus far employ only methods of pattern recognition in data. Be it textual or visual, conceptually all AI is trained on a slurry of data in which repetitive reading and interpretation of its binary digits allow patterns at a scale imperceptible to humans to be recognised. This becomes a new language of pattern: a language impenetrable to manual reading, but at a computational scale becomes understandable and replicable - this language describes only relationships between data, and not data itself. Pattern recognition is a cognitive advantage which allowed humans to flourish evolutionarily, but when scales of power consumption between human thought and contemporary high power computing are considered it is clear how computers can interrogate further the imperceptible detail of data patterns. This makes a particularly effective predictor when tasked with only absorbing and interpreting data, and is being used in meteorological and medical contexts with great success.

Reading and interpreting data is only one side of the coin. Image generators externalise their interpretation of vast datasets through a 'generation frame', traditionally in a 1:1 square format: analytically a perfect, symmetrical, easily divisible work area of computational proportions. At total odds with tried and tested building blocks and systems of measurement which have been intimately derived by the human hand and of human proportion since the beginning of our built history. No part of the human body concerned with perceiving, moving through or interacting with the built environment, the foremost of which is the hand, is harmonious with the 1:1 proportion most favoured by the computer. Measurements, tools, materials and media throughout human history that have prevailed have largely been derived from anthropometric proportions. The most fundamental act of inserting ourselves as authors into the process of two-dimensional image generation is moulding it to our own proportionality, be this through cropping, stretching, extrapolation or repetition by hand. Juhani Palasmaa associates the tactile, sensory and full-body experience of spaces and objects with the importance of their tactile (human and hand-made) creation. [04] From a Palasmic standpoint, without human intervention an artificially generated design element cannot be experienced to the fullest extent of human sensoral perception. Any anthropomorphic qualities generated through computation are the result of a recognised pattern, an artifice relating to no particular body. Is the idea of 'embodied wisdom' in the impulse of the hand totally incompatible with design outputs from alternate intelligences?

We create with our head and our hands: the head logical, the hands impulsive. Computers can, and will, automate logical tasks where a binary of correct / incorrect are the clearly defined sole outcomes. I ask, can AI replicate and augment impulse?

A LUDDITE FALLACY

'*A Luddite Fallacy*' is a sneering economist's phrase used to disregard the idea of automation displacing human work at a large scale. Speculating on a near-future Grays, a periphery town to London around thirty miles downstream the Thames, I imagined such a 'fallacy' to become reality, and explored the systemic, aesthetic and social change that would have to accompany it. Positioned at the final stage of our existing hybrid relationship between AI and work, and mechanical automata having displaced all human warehouse and manufacturing labour, I experimented with working alongside AI as a co-producer to design a seat of government for this new model of city and society.

We are as much products of our environment as AI is a product of its dataset. Selectively feeding and

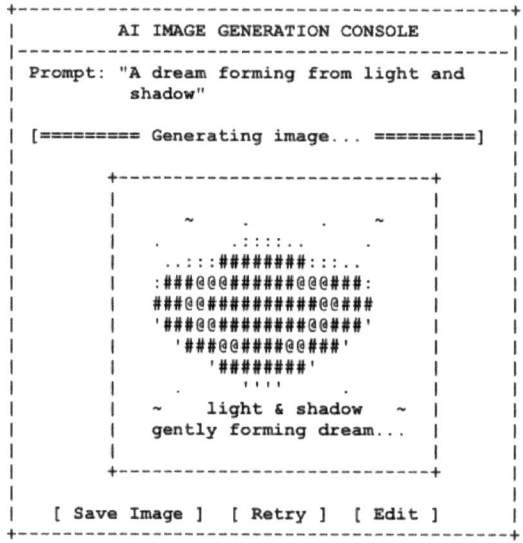

ASCII art of an AI generation dialogue, ChatGPT-4o

emphasising data points to an AI can streamline a process of intentional replica in order to function as a tool for optioneering. (St)architects are all too keen to deploy the napkin sketch, a product of their singular impulse and genius, as a seed which informs all facets of a years-long labour intensive process to produce a building. Narratively established as a singularity void of pre-thought or post-rationalisation which finds itself a visual touchstone for the labour of many - a single image and its author carries such power.

I sought to outsource the napkin sketch and re-align its usage. Starting with a series of my own sketches in black Pentel ink on 60g/m2 white trace, I assembled a small dataset. These sketches didn't appear out of the blue; they were informed both passively by my taste and lived experience to date, and actively by two walks fresh in my memory that interrogated and bound the industrial site (a soap factory), from both the mechanical scale of the river and the human scale of the town. Carrying snippets of embodied wisdom with which to invigorate the design process, these sketches served as the AI's initial touchstone.

I will avoid stressing the mechanics, which no doubt will be unrecognisable in years or even months to come, but will describe it in conceptual terms as clearly as possible. A low-rank adaptation (LoRA) process was used to interrogate the minutiae of my sketches, the subconscious patterns that the pen in my hand follows, and convert them into a stylistic guide with which new content can be generated. In combination with a descriptive text prompt and an input image, the LoRA executed a process of (re)/(mis)interpretation, overlaying a veneer of replica impulse which is illogical and non-contextual. As shown in Fig. D, varying levels of adherence to the text prompt and input image, defined by the human curator, allow more or less freedom for the AI to 'hallucinate' detail that relates to, but did not exist in, the input, dissolving human logic into digital noise. Re-drawing these outputs, of which an integral part is the application of design logic, began a conversation between the human designer and digital impulse-machine. I found that the tense discord between these two perspectives invigorates the design process, with digital impulse stimulating the human impulse much more than a traditional iterative process to reach an exciting composite endpoint. In this process, AI design is not so much a categorisable aesthetic as it is evidence of a back-and-forth, or a pushing and pulling, and demonstrably has augmented my design thinking.

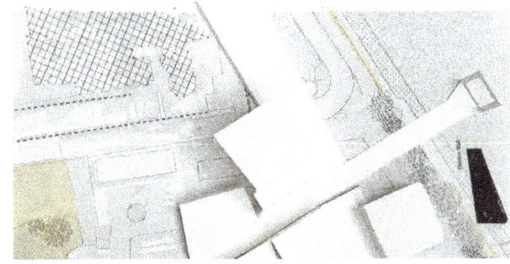

(Top to bottom) Original 'analog' input image followerd by layers of increasing AI abstraction / misinterpretation based on the author's impulse.

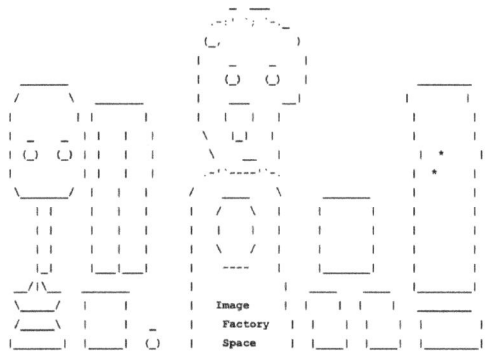

ASCII art of an image factory, ChatGPT-4o

TOMORROW'S IMAGE FACTORIES

Gordon Cullen's concept of serial vision, the idea that cities are experienced through movement, is not dissimilar to the thread and node method of reading a city. [05] Cullen proposes characteristics of urban places that make them pleasant to move through, such as enclosure, release, repetition, vistas and closures - such things occur only through intentional, combined stewardship of a city. It is clear that the introduction of AI will disrupt labour, and a shift in labour shifts the city that facilitates it - it is yet to be seen if a morphing townscape and landscape complete the cycle to shift the modes and goals of AI. Will we begin to see reciprocity between London and Grays, for example?

The link between image and space has been frequently addressed throughout the history of architecture. Fresco paintings as early as the fifteenth century would use forced perspective to indicate space beyond the terminating wall that they were applied to. In the late twentieth century, a tradition of adorning images as a facade treatment entered the wider architectural canon, which became developed and abstracted further with the parametricism of the 2000s. But in treating architectural plan, section and elevation drawings as images too, spatial qualities beyond planar appliqué can be affected by image. Many roles of the designer, and at large the white collar workforce, can be boiled down to creating 'images', a task that can be partially automated by AI. This is where I believe elements of Morris' factory of the future will begin to manifest in our society. Beyond fully automated mechanical automata, partially-automated image factories will house a majority of the workforce, fully capable of facilitating the utopian ideals Morris posited in his essays providing that economic and societal readjustment goes hand-in-hand with the change in work cultures.

To demonstrate on an urban scale, a design investigation expanding into the wider Grays/Tilbury belt speculated on what a town could become where social change did not follow full automation and old work cultures were carried into a new world, as well as allowing AI automation to flourish unchallenged by human impulse (Fig. G). Provoked by David Graeber's interrogation of the phenomenon of *Bullshit Jobs* in the workforce, [06] the project imagines Tilbury, a nearby industrial town to Grays on the Thames estuary, succumbing to societally ruinous culture around workplace automation. Clinging onto work cultures of the past, many people undertake an artificial commute to carry out pointless tasks, their 'work day' serving a purely social function, while civic responsibilities are automated by AI and completely unchecked by humans.

What remains is a dissolved and divided town, bisected by expressways for moving goods allowed by an automated town planning scheme. The borders exacerbate existing divisions in the town and create a new social hierarchy between 'bullshit workers', the many who retained old working cultures in the age of automation, and the 'free agents', the few who are emancipated from work life. At present Tilbury can be read similarly to the nineteenth century shipyard. Workers within the town are seldom free from the sight of the port or Amazon fulfilment centre, and follow short commutes - a basepoint from which to build upon through careful stewardship and collaborative automation. The division of the town and destruction of its threads in favour of artificiality leaves nothing but a floating slop of nodes resembling more free market commercial sprawl than a liveable urban environment.

In the automated factory of the future, both utilising and challenging our new alternate intelligences are of profound civic importance.

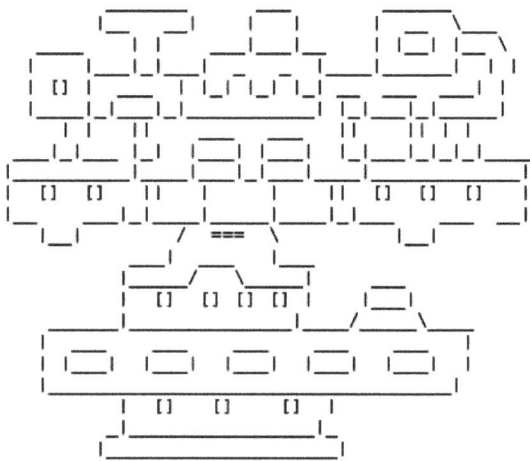

ASCII art of a disruped townscape, ChatGPT-4o

Notes

(01) William Morris, *A Factory as it Might Be I, II and III, Justice*, 1884. Articles for Justice: *"The Organ of the Social Democracy"*
(02) Edward H Lorenz, An Evolutionary Explanation for Competitive Decline: The British Shipbuilding Industry, 1890-1970, *The Journal of Economic History*, Vol. 51, No. 4 (Dec. 1991), pp. 911-935
(03) Adolf Loos, *Ornament and Crime*, Penguin, 2019 (Originally Published 1913), Translated by Shaun Whiteside
(04) Juhani Pallasmaa, *The Thinking Hand*, Wiley, 2009
(05) Gordon Cullen, *The Concise Townscape*, Architectural Press, 1961
(06) David Graeber, *Bullshit Jobs*, Penguin, 2018

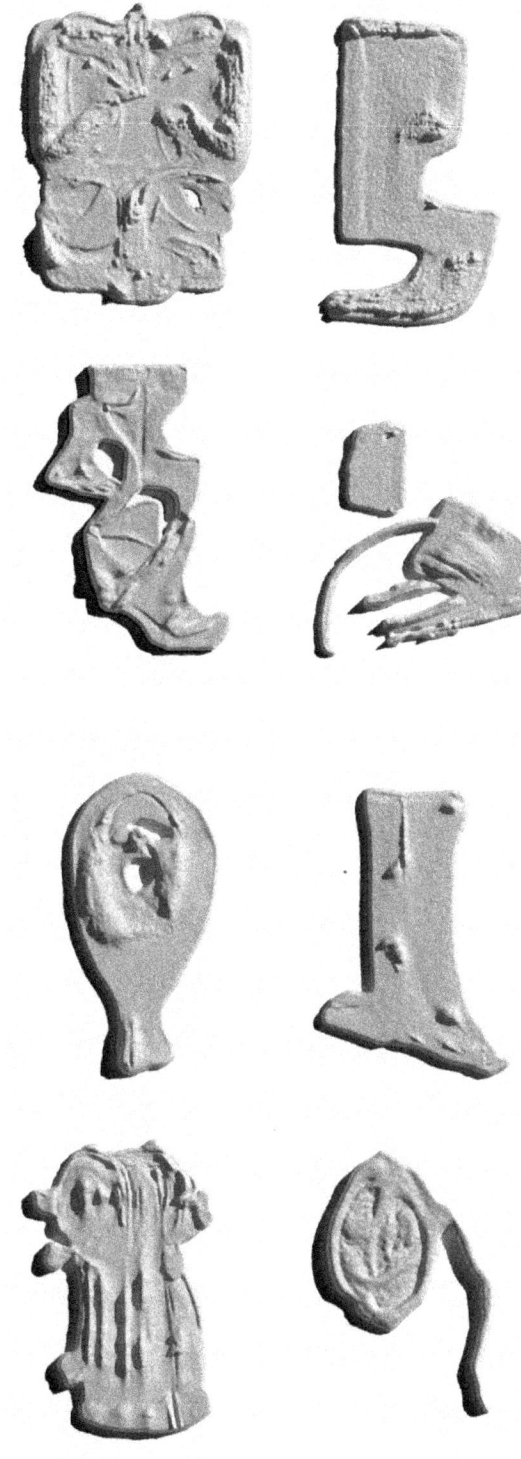

Hallucinated objects - derived from AI trained on Rhino .3dm model screenshots

A NEW DECENTRALAND

BODHI HORTON

This project confronts the growing divide between the affluence of emerging virtual worlds and the material decline of peripheral urban places. Regions like the Thames Gateway, burdened by the melancholic image of their industrial past, are being bypassed by the technologies of tomorrow, specifically the imminent rise of Web 3.0. The project interrogates this disparity, asking how the decentralised, community governed systems of this new internet could be harnessed to catalyse meaningful urban regeneration beyond the failures of current top-down models.

The project proposes a speculative model for urban revival situated in the fragmented landscape of Gravesend. Its central architectural intervention is a "virtual world embassy," a physical gateway that merges the town with its digital counterpart. This structure is not merely a building but a dynamic interface that integrates renewed local industry, ecological systems, and emergent technologies. Through this embassy, a virtual image of Gravesend is established and nurtured, creating new relationships between the physical environment and its digital representation. The design uses scenario-building to explore how this hybrid reality could reshape the town's identity, economy, and social fabric, moving from decay to techno-ecological vitality.

By creating a symbiotic feedback loop, the prosperity generated within the virtual image of Gravesend can be channelled back to repair the physical town. This model generates new, sustainable opportunities and challenges conventional development paradigms, suggesting a future where the virtual does not replace the real, but becomes a powerful catalyst for tangible, place-based renewal.

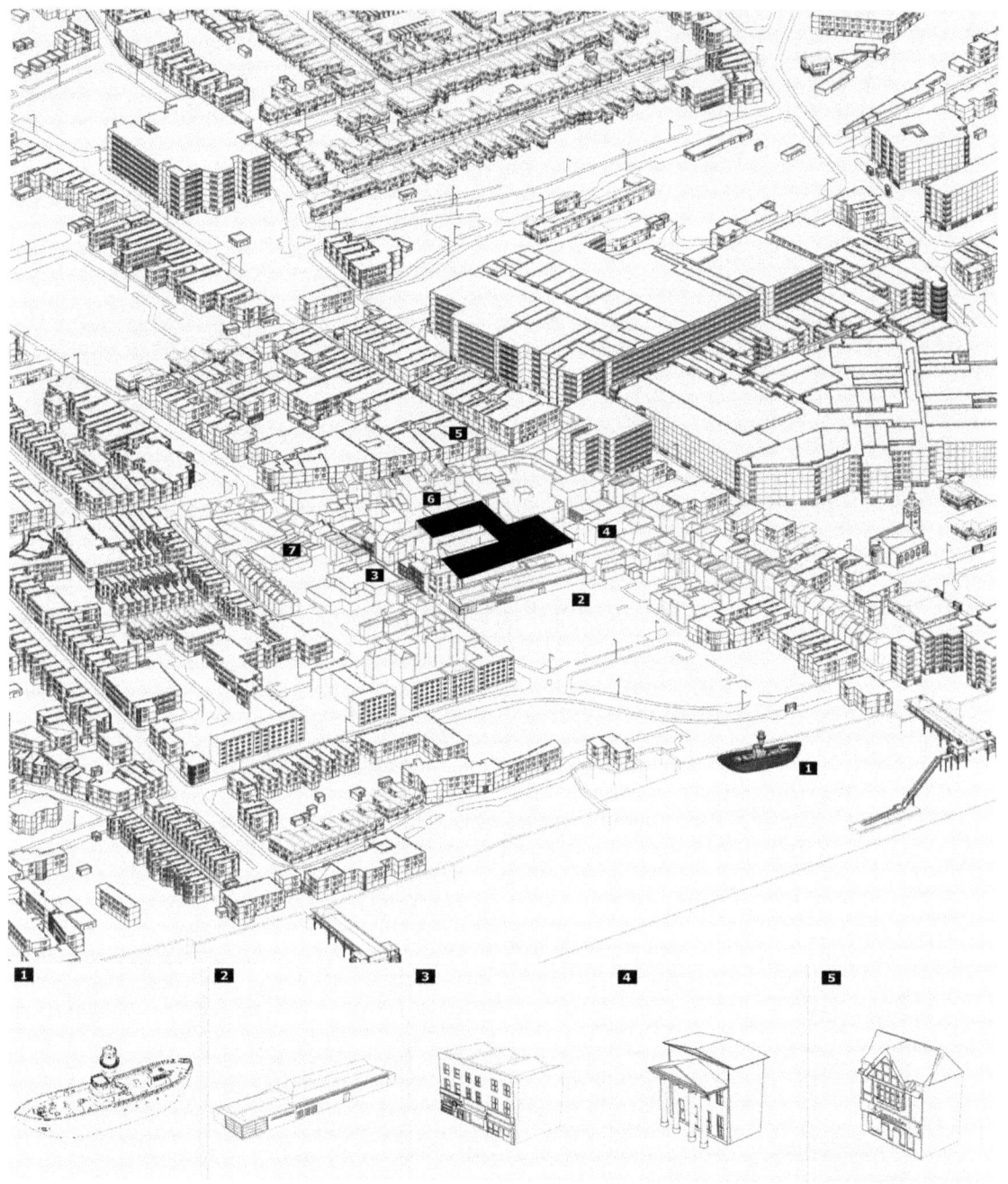

This project responds to an intensifying spatial inequality driven by capital-centric urbanism, leaving peripheries like the Thames Gateway in material decline while wealth accumulates in abstract digital economies. It critiques failing, top-down regeneration models that ignore the cultural and economic contexts of place.

Positioned within speculative architectural practice, the work challenges the escapist narrative of the metaverse. Instead, it draws from the decentralised principles of Web 3.0 to propose a form of cyber-urbanism, a hybrid model where digital and physical realities are mutually constituted. As society stands at the precipice of this new technological paradigm, this intervention is urgent. It speculates on a proactive role for architecture in shaping emergent digital worlds, aiming to forge symbiotic relationships that foster equitable, place-based renewal rather than exacerbating existing divides.

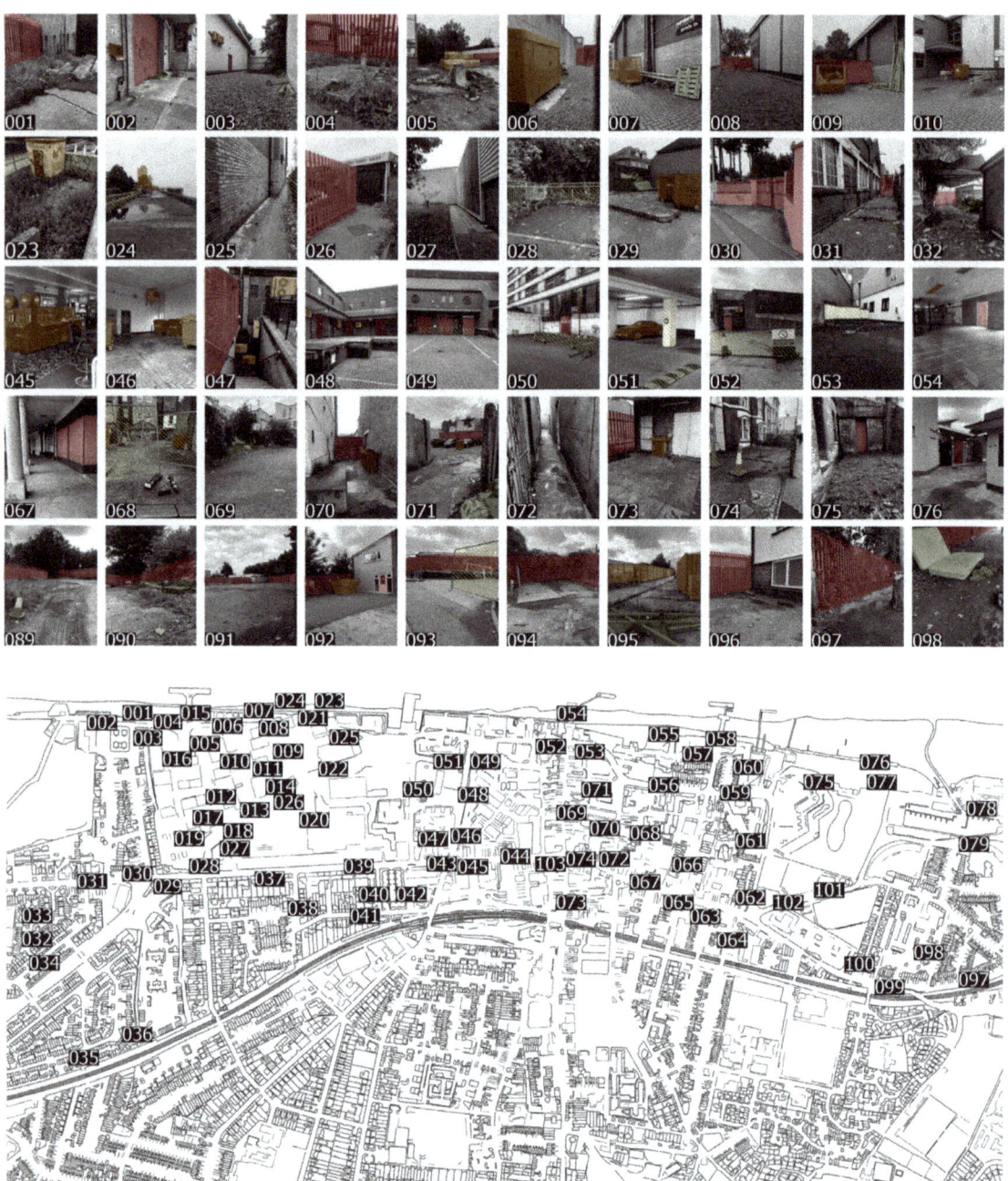

The project began with research into current regeneration efforts along the Thames Gateway. Using detailed context modelling, a kit of elements was developed, reflecting the town's identity and crafting a narrative for a digital overlay to enhance existing structures and attract investment. The design phase involved mapping embassy programs and blocking out a site-based proposal in Rhino. Through rigorous design iterations, the project shifted toward a narrative driven approach.

The final scheme was imported into Unreal Engine and combined with a procedural model of Gravesend created to produce an immersive digital environment. Real-time rendering and animated effects were used to convey the story of blockchain-led regeneration. The process was shaped by a guiding hypothesis: that digital overlays, driven by emerging technologies, can act as catalysts for renewed investment and regeneration in post-industrial towns.

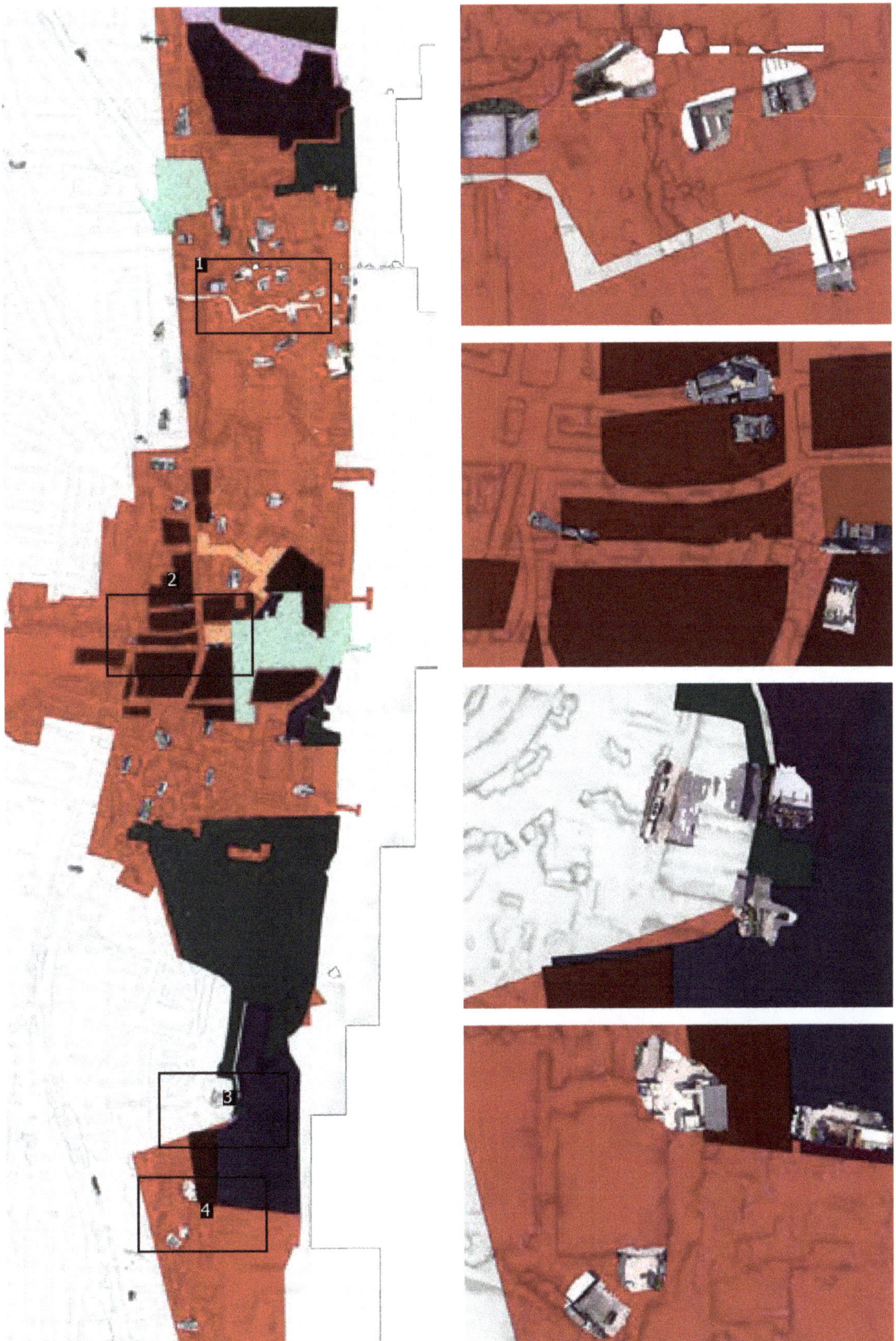

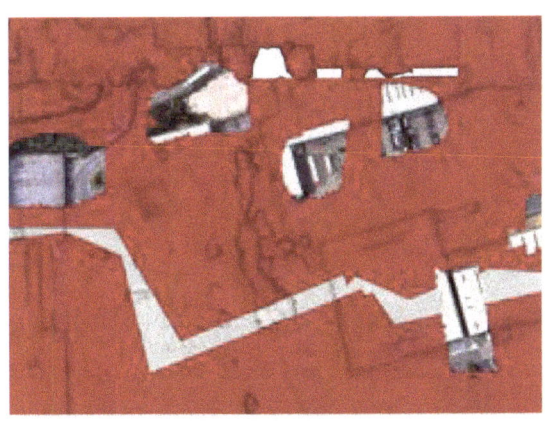
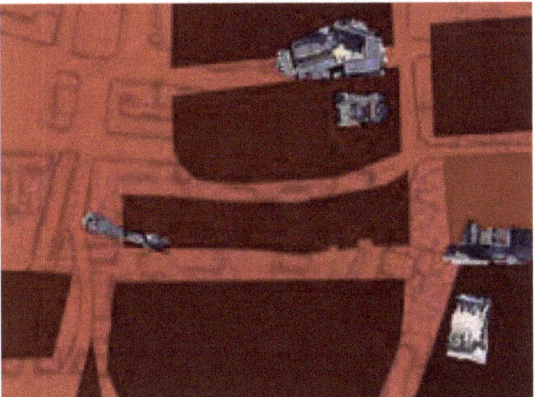
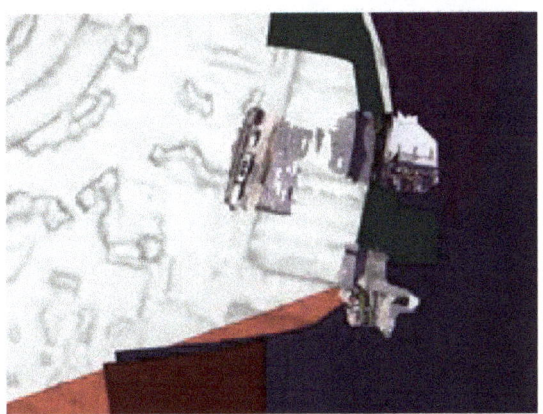
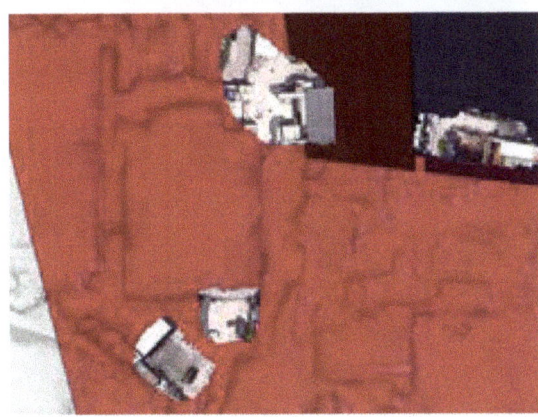

Project Images
Speculative embassy negotiating both a physical and digital presence embedded within the urban landscape of Gravesend.

195 - 199: Digital fragment and contextual recompositions
200 - 205: Design visualisations

A LUDDITE FALLACY

ERIC TURNER

A Luddite Fallacy proposes an alternative political system and way of living in Grays, Essex, enabled by increasing workplace automation.

The proposal is a new city hall for an independent, self-governing Grays, where the local community gains stewardship of the landscape and engages in debate over the construction, conservation and rewilding of the Thames estuary. An empty political testbed is left following the local council's 2022 bankruptcy, allowing an alternative economic system to be established. Situating itself between the Procter & Gamble soap factory and the 13th Century St Clement's church, the city hall acts as a base point for resistance against further industrialisation, mediating the boundary between production and conservation.

The building program responds to the neglect of the Thames riverbank by embodying three contrasting remedial approaches, which have been personified as characters:

1. *The 'Juror'* , a courtroom concerned with spatial justice, preserving public space and rights of way in the face of creeping industrial build-up.
2. *The 'Archivist'*, a multimodal archive concerned with the conservation of the existing and the uncovering of historical lines. The archive comprises physical storage, digital storage, and a large-format store room of salvaged surplus building components.
3. *The 'Landscape Gardener'*, the intermediate landscape/piazza between the proposal and it's context, its central point a debating chamber in which land usage is debated by the residents of Grays.

Materials are borrowed from fully automated factories nearby in accordance with the the 'automated landscape'. The use of these non-extractive materials describes a societal shift away from accelerationist principles and towards a sustainable, post-scarcity future.

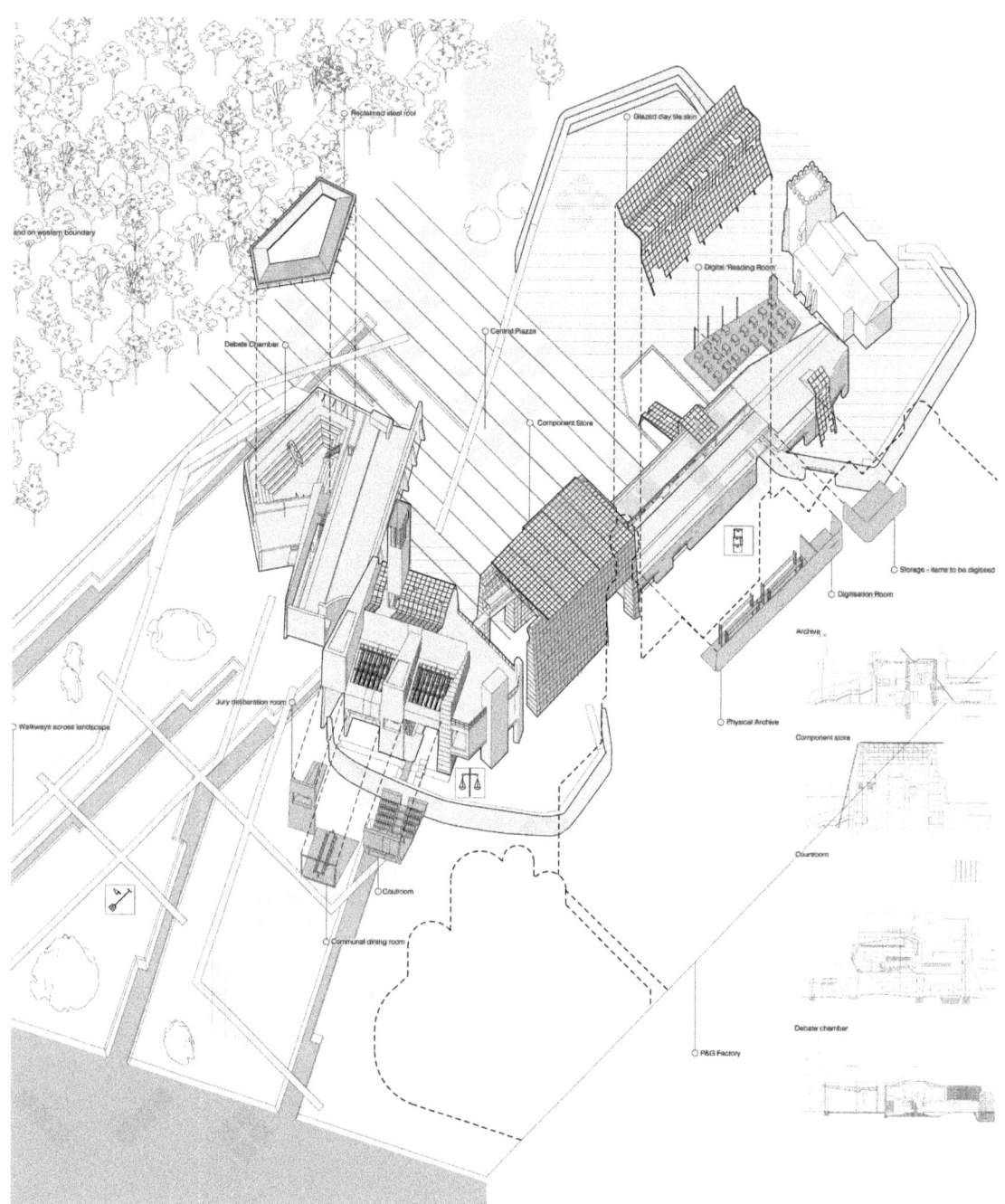

Grays and Tilbury are home to various manufacturing and logistics hubs such as the Tilbury Port and Amazon Fulfilment Centre. At odds with their towns, these highly automated spaces exist as scars in the landscape, serving London's demand for deliveries and goods in a non-reciprocal exchange. Can automation be used to the benefit of the people of Grays? Thurrock council's bankruptcy in 2022 is a clear indication that the existing political system is failing the area. Full automation can lead to a post-scarcity economic system such as Aaron Bastani's concept of *Fully Automated Luxury Communism,* emancipating workers from automatable work and allowing them time to engage with their urban environment. The concept of the *'automated landscape'* posits that fully automated workplaces can take on a radically reduced volume, no longer catering to human proportions.

The project tests generative AI and chance-based workflows, with AI as an inevitable collaborator/automator with/of the architect of the future. As an experiment in automating the design impulse embodied in the designer's hand (this embodied impulse a pallasmic theory), my own 'napkin sketches' informed by initial visits and responses to the site were used to train a Low Rank Adaptation (LoRA) AI model. The process of design involved treating architectural drawings as 'images', drawing initially by hand and then prompting the AI to re-draw / reinterpret the human impulse of iteration. Entering into this conversation between human and artificial thought encourages a subversion of typical thought processes, and re-drawing and applying spatial logic to an AI output often results in a tense yet exciting output. This process was applied to architectural drawings, models, digital media and prints, focussing on the AI's ability to misinterpret or 'hallucinate' elements that invigorate the design process.

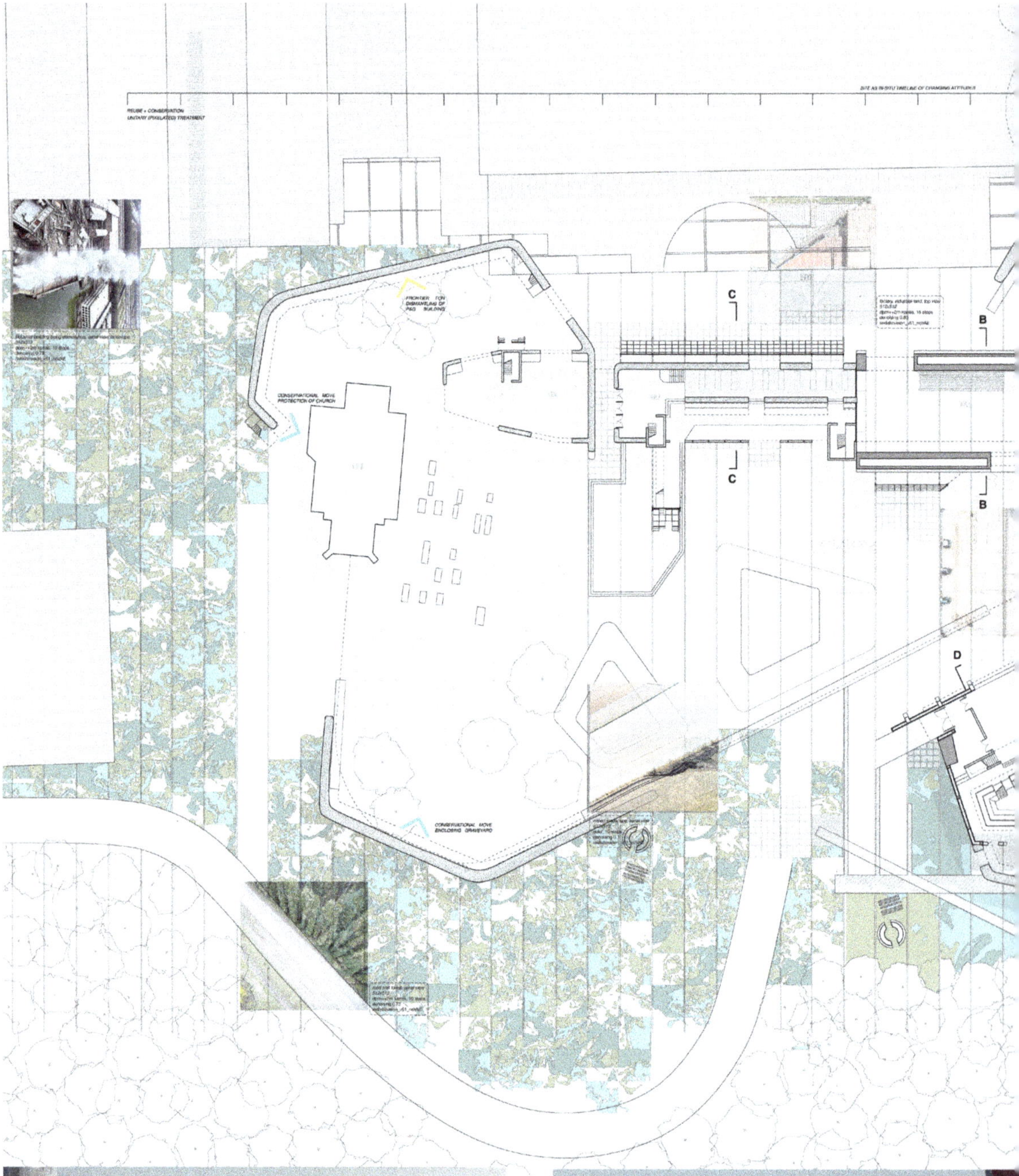

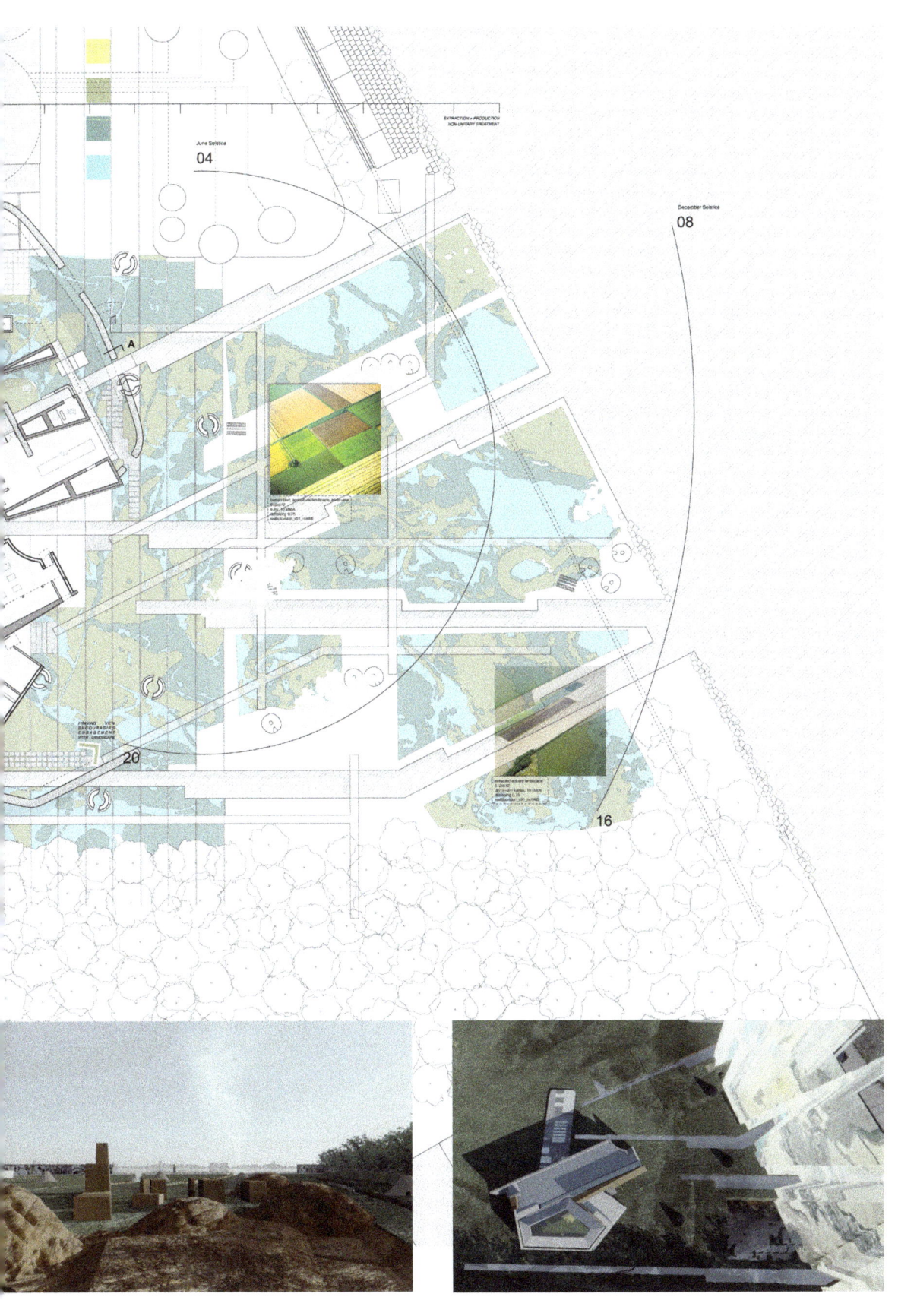

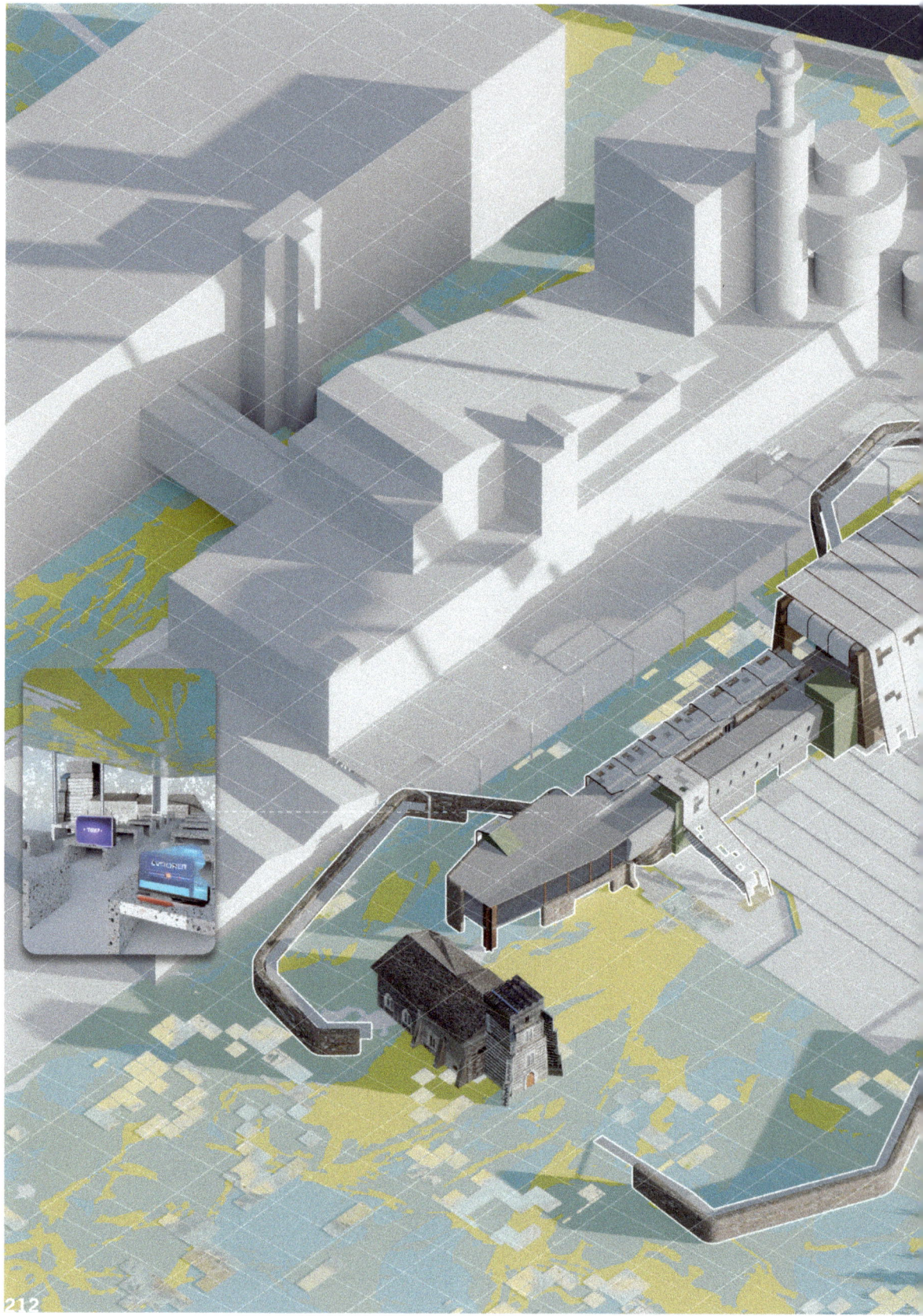

ENDPAPER

SUSANNAH HAGAN

The poetics of the relationships between the land and the humans occupying it, whether temporarily or permanently, have given rise in Studio 04 to some valuable responses from its students. They are indicative of an appreciation that although the unbuilt is empty of the built, it is full of something else – historical, cultural, personal and/or ecological. It is also indicative of a design studio responsive to what its graduates will be facing in the 21st century: the need to negotiate with natural systems in a state of flux if not collapse. The question for Studio 04 now is where it goes from here. Has it reached such a state of maturity, it has merely to reinforce what has already been achieved, or is there further to go? Once one enters the ecological arena, meeting the challenge of environmental free-fall in pedagogical terms can push us toward harder questions and more radical answers, though there's a lot stacked against acting on any of those answers.

Architectural education has so many moving parts, it's next to impossible to discuss it as a collective noun. 'Collective' it isn't. Instead, it is a number of disparate disciplines that can be crudely divided into the building sciences, history and theory (usually, though not always, of architecture), and of course, design. Beyond the basic requirements of professional validating bodies, these disciplines keep to their own languages and agendas, unable to agree on whether they are there to train students for practice or to explore.

Most teachers of architecture see the achingly obvious need to do both, though few if any schools deliver both in equal measure, let alone try to meld them into a coherent design training. Instead, subjects are still taught separately in a majority of architecture schools, allowed only guest appearances in the studio from other disciplines for specific projects. It is up to the student to integrate them in their personal approach to design, a hit and miss process that may or may not produce architects who are prepared for probably the most challenging century the built environment has so far faced.

These disciplinary 'silos' provide ample opportunity to diverge ever further from each other, speaking mainly to themselves. Cross-disciplinary alliances are usually supported only insofar as the group proposing them leads them. A studio initiative to bring in building science as more than simply the fulfilment of a bureaucratic requirement for technical input is rarely if ever allowed to influence the studio to the point where interdisciplinary thinking is deployed from the start of a project, though this happens in architectural practice.

Given what we face globally, enlaced environmental and housing crises – 'dwelling' in its broadest sense - it's clear that studio tutors, however dedicated, however brilliant, cannot encompass all the knowledge now essential for effective design thinking and practice. They need other contributions, not just in the studio on an ad hoc basis, but integrated with it so that designing becomes as effective as it is inventive. There are a few fascinating examples of new pedagogies in schools of architecture, but not yet a critical mass to ensure that engineer speaks unto historian, and designer speaks unto engineer as equal members of design studios concerned with better equipping students for their century.

The persistent 'If I ruled the world' approach to design projects is out of step with the times, producing end of year shows that are consequently more fine than applied art, with a hopelessly out of date emphasis on individual 'genius'. This may have been exciting in the past, but it won't work for the immediate future, which cries out for collaboration to successfully get us through this transition period, from a master-slave relationship with nature to a symbiotic one. If we manage it, and we still want to, we can then return to our silos, with their unequal distribution of status and resources.

The admirable Studio 04 raises another hard question, perhaps even harder, certainly larger: should one be speculating at all about newbuild on what is a vast water management system, a floodplain? Isn't its raison d'être to absorb floodwater and maintain the complex biotic interrelationships it is home to, and not to host yet more of our interventions? The studio work here has intervened first and foremost to protect and enhance the lives of local citizens. Since the 20th century, this has been one of architecture's primary roles. And yet in practices today, such assumptions have already been challenged in acknowledgement of an even greater, and one hopes temporary, imperative:

'There should be much, much less building… The only building that's justified is the renovation of existing structures … So maybe in the future we need fewer designing architects, and more thinking about resources, energy and sustainability policy, and spatial planning.'
– Adam Caruso, Caruso St. John Architects, 2020

Too many schools of architecture are nowhere near this kind of questioning of the current purpose of architecture and architectural education, let alone responded to it with epistemological and pedagogical change. Whether Studio 04's tutors and their students would want to address the questions raised here, or whether they'd be allowed to if they wanted to, they have creatively addressed the acute urgency of the crisis that faces us.

BIOGRAPHIES

Paolo Zaide is an architect, academic and curator and Course Leader for the BA Architecture Programme at the University of Westminster. His research, teaching and practice interests focus on the impact of future trends on contemporary cities. He explores this through the lens of ecological urbanism – urban design through an environmental lens – and has been responsible for co-curating public events and exhibitions in London and Hong Kong around the themes of ecologies in the city, including City Garden Follies in Camden Council (2010-13) and Visions 2050 Hong Kong Architecture and Urbanism Biennale (2015).

Tom Budd is an architect, visualiser and academic based in London. Since graduating from The Bartlett School of Architecture in 2018 Tom has worked at a variety of architectural practices, including Foster and Partners, Archio and Moxon. Tom currently splits his time between teaching, visualisation, design and research projects, running architecture and landscape design studios at both Westminster University and the Bartlett School of Architecture. In Tom's work and teaching there is a strong emphasis on the craft, skills and processes underpinning design practice, with a focus on challenging conventions and encouraging innovation through an exploratory approach.

Susannah Hagan is Emeritus Professor of Architecture at the University of Westminster, London, and a Fellow of the Royal Society of Arts. Prior to Westminster, she was Head of Research and the Doctoral Programme at the School of Architecture, Royal College of Art. She has published extensively, drawing together architectural design, history and theory to examine environmental practice in publications such as Digitalia (2008), Ecological Urbanism (2015) and Revolution? Architecture and the Anthropocene (2022)

Christine Hawley, Professor Emeritus of the Bartlett School of Architecture (UCL), has been the Head of two Schools of Architecture and Dean of the Bartlett. and was awarded the 2016 RIBA Annie Spink Award for excellence in architectural education. Her book 'Transitions' (2013) examines how conceptual threads begin to compose a specific architectural design 'language' and how ideas have both fluidity and the ability to transform.

ACKNOWLEDGEMENTS

This book would not have been possible without the support and contributions of many.

We wish to acknowledge the support of Harry Charrington, our former Head of School, Lindsay Bremner, Director of Research and Knowledge Exchange, and Victoria Watson and Will McLean for supporting this project. Thank you also to Mark Boyce for his work on the overall graphic design of the *Studio as Book* series.

We are especially grateful to Christine Hawley and Susannah Hagan for their inspirational mentorship and continued engagement with the ideas at the heart of this research.

We also wish to particularly thank the members of the studio whose written and visual contributions have enriched and inspired this work: Adelina Ivan, Axelle Sibierski, Bodhi Horton, Colin Walter, Eric Turner, Fenn Wright, Greg Brookhouse, Ioana Zavoianu, Marta Fernandes Contente, Pablo Pimentel, and Reece Murray. We greatly enjoyed the discussions and exchanges that helped bring the project together.

Special thanks to those whose images have helped illustrate and expand the narrative: Daniel Poshtovenko, Katarzyna Wojciechowska, Layla El Wadnakssi, Milan Lad, Oscar Chainey, Raoul Tomaselli, Sofia Rota, Yuan Padilla, and Yu-Rui Ray Hung.

- Paolo Zaide and Tom Budd

Blurs, Shifts & Edges

Design Studio 4
Edited by Paolo Zaide & Tom Budd

A University of Westminster,
School of Architecture + Cities Publication

Designed by Mark Boyce

All texts ©2025 the authors

This work is licensed under a CC BY-NC 4.0 license

ISBN 978-1-7385696-4-9

Books in the Studio as Book series are available to purchase via OpenStudioWestminster here: http://www.openstudiowestminster.org/studio-as-book/ or from online book stores.

The editors have attempted to acknowledge all sources of images used and apologise for any errors or omissions.

School of Architecture + Cities
University of Westminster
35 Marylebone Road
London
NW1 5LS

www.ingramcontent.com/pod-product-compliance
Lightning Source LLC
Chambersburg PA
CBHW060927170426
43193CB00023B/2984